THE BUDGET PROCESS

The Budget Process

A Parliamentary Imperative

DAVID G. MCGEE, QC

Commonwealth Parliamentary Association
with

LONDON • ANN ARBOR, MI

First published 2007 by Pluto Press
345 Archway Road, London N6 5AA
and 839 Greene Street, Ann Arbor, MI 48106

Commonwealth Parliamentary Association
Suite 700, Westminster House
7 Millbank, London SW1P 3JA

Copyright © 2007 Commonwealth Parliamentary Association

The right of David G. McGee to be identified as the author of this work has been asserted by him in accordance with the Copyright, Designs and Patents Act 1988

ISBN 978-0-7453-2774-7

Produced for the Commonwealth Parliamentary Association
and Pluto Press by
Chase Publishing Services Ltd, Sidmouth EX10 9QG, UK
Printed and bound in the European Union

Contents

Foreword	ix
Preface	xiii
Acknowledgements	xvii
1 Introduction	**1**
What is a 'budget'?	1
Phases of the budget process	5
2 Budget preparation	**7**
Preparing a budget	7
The context of budget preparation	8
Fiscal responsibility	10
Gender budgeting	12
Budget forecast constraints	15
Involvement in preparing a budget	16
Ministers	16
Members of Parliament	17
Legislative involvement	19
Civil society's involvement	22
Participatory budgeting	23
Budget strategy	26
Budget secrecy	31
3 Approval of the budget – the setting	**35**
Budget approval phase	35
Presentation of the budget	36

Time of presentation	37
Manner of presentation	39
Budget explanations	39
Contents of budget proposals	42
The form of approval required for a budget	45
Confidence of the legislature	46
Overall approval of a budget	47
Approval of the components of a budget	47
Approval of individual appropriations	49
Timing of budget approval	50
Limitations on the need for legislative approval	51
Public-private partnerships	53
Interim approvals	55
Subsequent budget approvals	57
Reversionary budgets	59
4 Approval of the budget – the legislative process	**61**
Resources available to legislatures in considering budget proposals	61
Budget offices	63
Consideration of budget proposals	66
Committee organisation	68
Conduct of estimates examinations	71
Amendment of the budget	77
5 Implementing the budget	**83**
Obligations to implement a budget	83
Implementation by members	86
Implementation by civil society	86
Reporting requirements	87
Election reporting	89
Transfer of appropriations	89
New spending	91
6 Evaluation of the budget	**93**
Auditing	94

Following up audits	98
Reporting	99
Legislative evaluation	104
Evaluating public-private partnerships	106
Role of committees	107
Process of committees	110
Unappropriated expenditure	113
7 The federal dimension and second chambers	117
8 Reflections	125
Appendix 1 Works consulted	133
Appendix 2 Participants in the CPA Budget and Financial Oversight Workshop, London, 8–10 November 2006	137
Appendix 3 Scrutinising public expenditures: assessing the performance of Public Accounts Committees	139
Index	171

Foreword

Several years ago at a Commonwealth Parliamentary Association (CPA) Regional Conference, a Parliamentarian from a Southern African country made a very frank admission. Soon after she entered Parliament she realised she lacked the knowledge about financial processes which she needed to do much of her parliamentary work. As a medical doctor, she was used to continuous learning at a professional level, so she promptly enrolled in a financial management course.

In the United Kingdom House of Commons in 2006, members of a senior parliamentary committee participated in a seminar to improve their knowledge of the principles and practices of financial accountability. David McGee, during his attachment to the CPA Secretariat to research and begin writing this book, was able to attend this seminar and inform MPs about financial scrutiny in the New Zealand House of Representatives, where he serves as its Clerk. These deliberations, in turn, informed his research and assisted him in writing this authoritative and comprehensive book on the role of Parliament in the financial processes of governance.

Had this book been available at the time, it would have been at the top of the required reading list for that Southern African physician-Parliamentarian. The fact that there was no such all-encompassing account, written from the perspective of someone experienced in the day-to-day operations of a Parliament, led the CPA to enlist David McGee to examine the role of Parliament in the determination and oversight of how public money is spent. Mr McGee had already written an important book for the CPA on one aspect of Parliament's financial role, so it was time to broaden the look at the wider picture.

The CPA was not alone in the genesis and production of this new book. We were strongly encouraged and supported by the World Bank Institute, and particularly by Dr Rick Stapenhurst, Public Sector Management Specialist, who is one of the contributors of a significant appendix in this book. The direct involvement of the World Bank in programmes to help governments around the world to improve their management of public funds had repeatedly drawn attention to the potential for Parliaments to play a stronger and more effective role in this process.

A very valuable initial contribution had been made at the beginning of this millennium with Mr McGee's first book for us. The CPA, again in partnership with the World Bank Institute, held a Study Group on the role of the Public Accounts Committee. This group of members, with extensive experience in the work of such committees in a representative body of Commonwealth Parliaments, produced a report, *The Overseers*, written by David McGee as its rapporteur and published for the CPA by Pluto Press. It is a definitive guide to the work of Public Accounts Committees which has been used by the CPA and the World Bank Institute to enhance the roles of these key committees and similar bodies in Parliaments not just around the Commonwealth but around the world.

The CPA is proud to join with Mr McGee, the World Bank Institute and Pluto Press in publishing a volume which takes the role of Parliaments in financial management much further. This book examines how Parliament fulfils every step of one of its most fundamental authorities – the approval of the spending of public money on the governance of the people – and how Parliaments in diverse Commonwealth jurisdictions are developing practices and procedures to strengthen the effectiveness of this approval process as a major contributor to good governance and to development. Mr McGee's work clearly demonstrates that Parliaments are moving beyond their scrutinising role as the watchdog of the public purse to take a more active position in contributing to the financial management of their governments and their countries.

It is a book which all Members of Parliament around the world should read if, like our Southern African physician-Parliamentarian, they are to truly understand how Parliaments can play their full and rightful role in an area critical to the development of all countries, public finance.

Dr William F. Shija
Secretary-General
Commonwealth Parliamentary Association

Preface

In 2001 the Commonwealth Parliamentary Association sponsored a workshop in Toronto to discuss Public Accounts Committees. The workshop led to the publication of a book, *The Overseers*, discussing the operation of Public Accounts Committees in Commonwealth legislatures and the work of Auditors-General and other public audit officials in contributing to that work.

This book follows up that study by attempting an overview of the entire budget authorisation process that culminates in the examination of a state's financial operations by the Auditor-General and a Public Accounts Committee, as well as discussing aspects of the latter process (though not in the same detail as in *The Overseers*). This is a subject that has exercised the CPA before. In December 2001 the CPA sponsored a workshop held in Kenya that reported on parliamentary oversight of finance ('Ensuring Accountability in Public Expenditure' published in November 2002).

The budget process is, as will be appreciated, a much wider and more complex process than that dealt with in *The Overseers*. The procedures employed, indeed, the aims of the endeavour, are more disparate than those in respect of Public Accounts Committees. For the latter there is a great deal of commonality of organisation and agreement on objectives between legislatures, almost all of which employ processes of audit and review of a government's financial operations.

But for the process that leads to the expenditure authorities being granted and for those authorities being utilised there is a much greater degree of variation in the way that legislatures operate. Not only do they operate differently, the effect of their operations (or non-effect in some instances) differs markedly depending upon the political circumstances of the state involved. Different views are held about the purposes of the processes employed even where these are superficially similar. There are differences too in how the results of the process are regarded by internal and external observers, differences that may reflect fundamentally conflicting views of the object of the exercise. For these reasons an analysis of the budget process in different Parliaments is not a straightforward exercise.

However, this is not an admission of despair. Discussion of the budget process can be more than just a description of that process country by country. It can, by identifying differences of approach and effect, help to throw light on the consequences of choices that governments and legislatures make in regard to their budget practices. It can too, at a certain level of generality, reveal means of enhancing the effectiveness of those practices.

This book is an attempt to distil from budget practices an outline of what these are intended to achieve (and what they are not intended to achieve) and to make some tentative assessments of how effectively these goals are put into effect. Its central thesis is to regard the budget process as an aspect of governance and that therefore in order to promote good governance it is essential to have appropriate and effective rules and practices in place.

Given the disparate nature and objectives of budget processes, it is hazardous for an outside observer to make recommendations for specific changes to these. Where ideas for improvement do emerge they need to be identified by politicians, officials or other interested persons in the state concerned, rather than being specifically addressed to it. But it is hoped that this book will promote reflection on means by which the budget process can be enhanced in particular states.

This book is largely concerned with the contribution that *legislatures* make to the budget process. Apart from the occasional excursus to the sub-national level (for example, to discuss the federal dimension and participatory budgeting) it concentrates on national budgeting. It is not a work of research. The treatment is impressionistic rather than analytical. Only a narrow range of secondary resource material has been consulted and examples are taken from a few countries rather than a comprehensive review (see Appendix 1 for works consulted). Examples from non-Commonwealth legislatures have been cited where these have been judged applicable.

Because, in practice, legislatures are not engaged with the entire budget process and other persons and bodies outside Parliament and government make distinctive contributions to budget outcomes, the discussion in the book has not been entirely confined to the work of Parliament and Members of Parliament. But these are central to the aims of this book and extensive discussion of the work of persons outside the parliamentary environment has not been attempted. Such contributions must await a definitive study of how a budget is devised, adopted and implemented.

David McGee
July 2007

Acknowledgements

A study of this nature was conceived in discussions with the Hon. Denis Marshall, then Secretary-General of the Commonwealth Parliamentary Association, and Andrew Imlach, the Association's Director of Information Services. I would particularly like to thank them for their encouragement and assistance in making this project possible and for the continuing support of the CPA Executive Committee, chaired by Hon. Hashim Abdul Halim MLA, and the current Secretary-General, Dr William F. Shija. This support allowed me to spend some ten weeks at the Association's headquarters in late 2006 researching material and beginning work on writing the book. During this time too I was able to participate in a Budget and Financial Oversight Workshop organised by the Association at which a number of the issues discussed in this book were debated (see Appendix 2 for a list of participants).

While in London I was fortunate to occupy an office courtesy of the Department of the Clerk of the House. I am very grateful to the department and, in particular, to Helen Irwin, Clerk of Committees, for the very generous assistance provided to me over this period. Amongst other things I was able to participate in departmental activities and discuss ideas relevant to this work with clerks in the department. A particularly valuable experience was attending and giving evidence to the Liaison Committee of the House of Commons during a hearing it held on a Hansard Society report that was very pertinent to my study.

I would like too to thank the Speaker of the House of Representatives, New Zealand, the Hon. Margaret Wilson, for agreeing to my absenting myself from my duties for the period that I spent at the Commonwealth Parliamentary Association.

In the writing of the book I owe a particular debt of gratitude to the Parliamentary Library, New Zealand, for the assistance that it has provided to me in identifying materials. I want to acknowledge the collaborative assistance of Pleasance Purser and John Wilson of that library, not only for their efforts in finding materials of use to me but for the feedback that they have provided during the writing of the book. Their assistance has been invaluable.

Finally, I would like to thank Luseane 'Ofa Chesham of the Commonwealth Parliamentary Association and Jo Shepherd, Secretary to the Clerk of the House, for the help that they gave me in working on this project in, respectively, London and Wellington. This has also been much appreciated.

1
Introduction

WHAT IS A 'BUDGET'?

In most legislatures (in bicameral legislatures, in the lower House) the presentation of a budget will be the major annual parliamentary event. The budget's delivery is a quintessential parliamentary occasion, widely anticipated, attracting speculation, possible drama and extensive political analysis. Referring to 'the budget' is commonplace. But what do we actually mean when we use the expression 'the budget'? It is necessary at the outset of a study of this nature to reflect on what the term 'budget' actually signifies.

Originally, the word 'budget' meant the pouch or bag in which the British Treasurer carried state documents relating to financial matters. Something of that sense of the word is recalled in the practice of British Chancellors of the Exchequer posing for photographs outside their official residence in Downing Street carrying the budget speech in a red despatch box before going to the House of Commons to deliver it. The despatch box represents the 'budget' understood in its original sense. (The despatch box in use until quite recently was first used by William Gladstone around 1860. A new budget box was put into use in 1997 having been made for the Chancellor by young trainees in his constituency.)

More commonly, the term 'the budget' refers to an event as referred to above. It is the statement of the government's economic and fiscal measures to the legislature on an appointed day (budget day). Most people would probably understand the budget in this sense and it is this tangible event that is the premier parliamentary occasion each year. Associated with this meaning of an event, it has been common to regard the budget as the actual document in which those measures are contained (and not just the bag in which they were carried). Thus, in the Netherlands the term 'budget' is used broadly to mean a budget memorandum and 23 associated budget bills.

The budget's importance in the latter senses of the word is that the statement or document tends to contain the most important decisions, at least of an economic or financial nature, that a government will make each year. In aggregate, this is certainly the case. But there is, even in countries that by law require such an annual statement, no necessity that this should be so. A government could tell the legislature in its budget statement that it had no policies to announce this year. Nevertheless, the level of expectation engendered by a budget and the opportunity of capturing public attention that it presents to a government, invariably makes it the case that significant economic and financial decisions are reserved for announcement as part of the budget.

Later in this book these aspects of the budget as an event and as a set of documents will be more fully discussed.

The term 'budget' has, however, taken on a wider meaning than these and this meaning is not specific to a parliamentary context, as are the previous senses that have been discussed.

This further meaning relates to the role of a budget, in any context, as a plan for an organisation's financial transactions over a future period. It is a means of projecting ahead to ensure that expenditure is covered by income, or, if not, that any shortfall is met from alternative sources such as reserves or borrowings. A budget is a plan that any prudent organisation will prepare. For a nation state it is seen as an essential element of governance to produce such a plan, though this was not always the case.

The growth of the budget as a means of organising decisions into a plan for the future has been traced to the English Parliament's acquisition of power to make significant taxation and expenditure decisions (Schick 2001). (Until the seventeenth century the executive – the Crown – still had significant taxation and expenditure authority of its own.) Made originally in an unorganised or ad hoc way, it was the organisation of these parliamentary decisions into a unified system by the government, rather than by the legislature itself, that created a budget for the nation. National budgeting in an historical sense is thus a function of the government. In most countries it still is.

This forward-looking and comprehensive aspect of a budget is, for many, its most interesting and significant aspect. A budget is a means of setting out a blueprint of a nation's economic and fiscal development for a defined future period of at least a year ahead. This involves an explanation of revenue-raising measures that the government intends to pursue in the period ahead and disclosure of the government's proposals for public expenditure. A budget in this sense is a statement of financial intentions. But increasingly absorbed into these projections are announcements with wider socio-economic significance. Drawing up a modern budget is an exercise in devising policy on an across-the-board basis. It is not the only or exclusive occasion on which policy, even fiscal policy, is announced, but it is the single most important one.

The budget then, can be seen as a plan embodying policy proposals disclosed to the legislature. Simply as a plan it carries no particular weight except such that can be imparted to it by a government's political strength. But to regard a budget as solely aspirational and contingent would, in most cases, be to understate its political significance. As will be seen, in most cases that plan will be formally endorsed and implemented. Any consideration of the budget's status needs to recognise this as a political fact. The budget then has also been regarded as an authoritative government *decision* on the priorities identified in the plan and on the policies that it contains (ibid.). This follows from the fact that in most Commonwealth legislatures approval of the budget is routine – defeat of a budget (in itself an unusual and unexpected event) causing a government to resign. It is indeed the case that a budget is such an integral aspect of governing that it is hard to see how a government that could not gain parliamentary endorsement for its budget could be said to be governing at all. However, there are differences in political systems in the Commonwealth that qualify the extent to which approval of a budget automatically follows its presentation to the legislature. These differences will be discussed later in this work.

All of the above meanings of the term 'budget' have their validity and require examination in their turn. But there is a final sense in which the term is used. That is as a *process* (in part, a legal process) involving a cycle, rather than as a single event, a document or even a plan, although all of these ideas can be encompassed as part of that process. A budget as a statement to the legislature has a genesis, it is examined by the legislature and, once approved, it is put into effect. Later the implementation of the measures it contains can be scrutinised for probity and efficiency. In this way 'the budget' can be seen as a lengthy process involving the government (ministers and officials), the legislature (including legislative officials such as the state's auditor – the Auditor-General), and other groups and persons who might contribute views on it during the course of that process. It was this emphasis on the budget as a process, for example, that led the Zambian estimates committee in 2004, in its first report after it was established, to consider the entire budget procedure from a legislature's perspective and come up with substantial recommendations for reform (Burnell 2001). (This report led to a number of changes in the way that the legislature considers budget proposals. Recommendations in the report that require constitutional amendment are under consideration as part of a constitutional review process.)

While it is useful for descriptive purposes to identify a single budget process, in reality a number of budget processes will be under way simultaneously. While a budget is being initiated for a future year, the current year's budget may be under examination by the legislature or may be being implemented. Even budget cycles relating to previous years may not have run their course since those budgets may be still under evaluation by the legislature and the Auditor-General. Governments and Members of Parliament will thus be engaged at different points of different budget processes during the course of the same year. Budget processes are dynamic and are always unwinding.

Tracking budget practices as part of a process or cycle is the approach that is followed in this book. Consideration of 'the budget' as an event or series of documents, and the intent of that event or those documents as a plan or effective decision will be considered in the context of that process. It must be admitted, however, that the other meanings of the term 'budget' make it difficult consistently to avoid using it in its other understood senses, without adopting artificial terminology. This temptation will not always be resisted.

PHASES OF THE BUDGET PROCESS

There are generally accepted to be four major phases in a budget process. As linear progressions in the processing of a budget these phases are followed in this book. (Though it must be conceded that not all countries would regard the fourth phase identified here – evaluation – as part of the budget process at all.) These phases are:

- preparation – the phase in which the package of economic and fiscal measures generally associated with an annual budget is devised;
- approval – the phase in which budget measures are announced and presented to the legislature for formal endorsement and in which they are given legal effect;
- implementation – the phase (which may begin before formal endorsement is given) in which budget measures are put into effect;
- evaluation – the post hoc auditing and scrutinising of the public sector's operations, originally to assure that those were strictly in accordance with legal authorisations, but increasingly to test against other performance yardsticks of efficiency and effectiveness.

These phases will be examined in turn, with particular emphasis on the role of legislatures at each point.

2
Budget preparation

PREPARING A BUDGET

Preparing a budget is regarded, without exception, as a function of the executive. In parliamentary systems only the executive is seen as having the capacity to undertake the complex process of putting a budget together. Indeed, this function may be explicitly conferred on the executive by the Constitution or other law of the state concerned. In Uganda, for example, the Constitution vests the preparation of the budget in the President, who normally delegates the task to the Minister of Finance. In Madagascar the preparation of the budget is, under the Constitution, carried out under the authority of the Prime Minister by the Minister of Finance. But the primacy of the executive in budget preparation does not depend on such provisions. Rather they reflect the reality that budget preparation is an inherently executive function. It is therefore appropriate that the executive should take the lead in performing this duty.

Even in a country with a strong doctrine of the separation of powers such as the United States of America, the executive initiates the budget. In the United States, the legislature has the authority and (through the resources of the Congressional Budget Office) the capacity to reject the executive's budget and substitute one of its own, though this would be an unprecedented event. A consequence of this strong independence of the legislature from the executive is that Congress may become a forum to which public officials appeal to reverse budget preparation decisions taken within the executive. For example, the United States Army's chief of staff has been reported as refusing to make the budget cuts demanded by the United States Administration and testifying directly to Congress as to the army's needs.[1]

But a legislature with the capacity to act directly contrary to the wishes of the executive and to assume responsibility for budget preparation itself is not found in a parliamentary system or even in most systems with an executive President. Consequently contention between members of the executive over budget preparation is likely to be played out within the executive itself rather than before the legislature.

The extent to which executives consult with and involve others, particularly legislators, in the preparation of the budgets will be discussed below. But first it is necessary to consider some of the contextual factors that impinge on budget-making from an executive's point of view.

The context of budget preparation

Framing a budget is a political act. Its preparation will reflect the political climate within which a particular government has to operate. This will vary from country to country and, within any country, it will vary from time to time, depending on factors such as the government's legislative majority (if it has one), its standing in the community at large and the proximity of the next election.

Economic circumstances are further obvious constraints (or enabling factors) on the budget choices that a government can make. In countries with a heavy dependence on the export prices obtained for a particular commodity (such as Trinidad and Tobago in respect of oil) movements in those prices will be a major factor in determining what economic and fiscal policies are practicable. Indeed, countries may adopt formal fiscal constraints in their budget decisions that are dependant upon export price movements. Thus in Chile a government rule mandates a budget surplus of 1 percent

---

1. 'Army chief defies Rumsfeld in bitter budget cuts row', *Daily Telegraph*, 26 September 2006.

of gross domestic product (GDP) if the copper price is at its long-term forecast level and the economy is growing at its underlying potential rate.[2] Anticipated currency movements may necessitate budget restraint where this would not otherwise exist. In a country with a heavy dependence on aid, budgetary decisions will in large measure be conditioned by the wishes of donors or lenders. In Zambia the chairperson of that country's National Economic Development Council has been reported as complaining that Zambia's dependence on foreign aid meant that its own institutions could not freely decide on the expenditure of funds.[3]

It is also the case, especially in developed countries, that a great deal of budget decision-making is locked in by prior commitments. A large part of government expenditure is accounted for by 'entitlements', that is, payments or transfers that persons or groups are entitled to if they meet prescribed conditions – retirement pensions and other social security benefits, grants, interest and debt repayments, and so on. Governments, at least in the medium term, have little or no discretion in regard to these matters. They have to be reflected in budget preparation and they have to be funded. In this sense budgets become largely a means of accounting for the consequences of past decisions. They are the result of political trade-offs and adjustments made over the course of decades. For this reason the budget process has been adjusting its horizon beyond an annual timeframe and looking at medium- and long-term trends.

In federal systems particularly (but also in unitary states with significant sub-national governments) transfer payments from the federal to the state or provincial level may be a standing charge on the national treasury. In Canada such transfers are prescribed in legislation that is supplemented by agreements between federal and provincial finance ministers. In Australia, transfers of funds are made pursuant to an agreed formula as a percentage of goods and services tax receipts, thereby removing this factor (no doubt for good reasons of equity and predictability) from a government's control. Such accommodations between the different levels of government

2. 'Corseted', *The Economist*, 27 January 2007.
3. *Africa News Service*, 27 July 2004.

may thus be embodied in legal instruments or in standing agreements. Other countries may leave this entirely to political negotiation and accommodation between the different levels of government.

These matters bring a mix of external and internalised constraints to bear on a government's freedom to prepare a budget. In Canada, for example, some 70 percent of government spending is locked-in in these ways (Blöndel 2001a). But there are other matters of a policy or institutional budgetary nature that impinge on governments that also deserve to be mentioned. These factors, whether embodied in law or not, form a body of theoretical thinking about budget-making that, in an interdependent world, governments need to take into account in preparing their plans.

Fiscal responsibility

Increasingly states are adopting constraints of a macro-economic nature on a government's ability to frame a budget. These are seen as being desirable in introducing a measure of stability into economic management, rather than leaving this wholly to the discretion of governments which are perceived as likely to be driven by short-term electoral considerations. These constraints are the fiscal policy equivalents of the trend to hand control of monetary policy over to independent central banks.

In legal terms these constraints often take the form of fiscal responsibility legislation requiring that the consequences of fiscal and other economic policies contained in a budget be made explicit in reports to be prepared on budget measures and further requiring that departures from good fiscal practice (as variously defined) be accounted for and explained. A notable forerunner of this was legislation passed in New Zealand in 1994. While these legal requirements may not formally prevent governments proposing measures that would lead to fiscal deficits (though they may do this too), they can be a powerful factor in dissuading governments from proposing such policies, given the public exposure of the consequences of them that the mandatory fiscal reporting should ensure.

Less commonly, legislation may actually require a government to prepare a budget that is balanced in regard to its expenditure and revenue proposals according to definitions and exceptions described in the legislation. Most Canadian provinces have opted for this formal approach, though with varying degrees of flexibility and sanctions for not meeting fiscal targets. In other jurisdictions, rather than legislating for a balanced budget, this goal may be adopted as an express fiscal policy that has to be followed. At the federal level Canada and India have adopted this course.

Closely akin to these overall rules is the adoption, as a matter of policy, of budget targets either for a single year or over a longer budget cycle. Canada has had a 'no deficit rule' in effect since the 1997–98 fiscal year. Under this rule Canadian governments seek to produce budgets that will not allow fiscal balances to go into deficit. From 2004, they will aim to reduce the debt to GDP ratio from 41 percent to 25 percent over ten years (Beaumier 2006). Chile engages in counter-cyclical budgeting by aiming for a fiscal surplus if copper prices are strong and permitting a fiscal deficit if they are weak.[4] In these cases of policies of budgetary responsibility, the sanction is not one provided by law, it is political – the criticism or embarrassment that a government would face in failing to meet the target of a balanced budget or other standard even when this is self-imposed. Indeed, it is possible that over time such policies of budgetary rectitude could become conventions that governments are expected to follow as a matter of course, without needing to be re-endorsed by each new government. In this way, although not justiciable as matters of law, they would become part of the state's constitutional background against which budgets are prepared.

How effective such rules and policies are is a matter of contention. An Organisation for Economic Co-operation and Development (OECD) study has been reported as finding that budget balance rules were more effective if combined with rules to limit expenditure, so that extra revenues are not automatically spent as they might be

---

4. See footnote 2.

if fiscal balances were all that mattered. Budget balance rules not linked to expenditure limits have been less successful.[5]

But overall such policies are seen as contributing to responsible governance practices.

Gender budgeting

An important means of conceptualising the budget process that has developed over the last 30 years or so takes the form of considering its different impacts on men and women. The approaches to thinking about the budget in these terms are often referred to as gender budget initiatives. The initiatives take two broad forms: firstly, in analysing budgets for their underlying gender impacts and, secondly, in proposing the adoption of budgets with explicit gender-related goals.

Gender budget initiatives take as their starting point unequal relationships between men and women in society (and between and within other groups such as children, different ages, races, classes, and so on). However, although unequal relationships exist, they are not necessarily explicitly acknowledged or immediately apparent. They may consist of implicit assumptions about roles or be disguised by 'neutral' laws or policies that in practice favour one gender or group over another. Indeed, as more overt forms of discrimination are removed from the law, unequal relationships are increasingly confined to these 'hidden' forms. There may be limited information on inequality. Thus much statistical or economic data may fail to recognise the contribution that women in particular make to the economy through their disproportionate shares of household, voluntary and other unpaid work (though data are improving in this regard).

Gender budget initiatives become part of a programme of promoting equal rights in a practical as well as a legal sense and can be subsumed into general human rights developments. Governmental budgets, being important, indeed central, features of

---

5. 'Words of warning', *The Economist*, 26 May 2007.

BUDGET PREPARATION

economic strategy, have been the focus of particular thinking about how they can be used to advance these social goals. While particular policies advocated as part of gender budgeting may seek to target women specifically, the ultimate goal of proponents of gender budget initiatives is to build gender-consciousness into the underlying formulation of budgets. In this way a principal objective of government budgeting (and other governmental practices) would be to promote true equality between genders and between other groups in society (Balmori 2003).

The first gender budgeting initiatives were introduced in Australia (Bishop 2006). In the early 1970s units were established within government to provide for policy analysis of issues from a gender perspective. In 1984 equity analyses linked to the budget were introduced and women's budget statements began to be produced. From these beginnings gender budget initiatives have developed at the national and sub-national level in many countries. A recent review summarised activities in 42 countries, 17 of which were Commonwealth countries (Budlender 2001). However, the extent and impact of these initiatives differ considerably between the countries concerned (indeed, over time they have differed within the same country).

Gender budget initiatives are intended to contribute to the formulation of a gender-conscious budget whose components recognise and address the contributions and needs of the different genders. They tend to do this by concentrating on the analysis of the impacts or potential impacts of budget policies; asking what effects they have or would have on women. Thus even though a policy may be ostensibly neutral in its effects, its incidences may fall very differently on men as opposed to women. For example, in South Africa that country's land reform programme has been identified as potentially increasing gender inequalities, especially in poorer rural areas. This is because legal and customary restrictions have impeded women's access to land and prevented them obtaining the financial resources needed to develop it. Making land available on an unrestricted basis without removing existing legal and social restrictions on women holding land and then directing resources towards them so that they could use land productively, will mean that they are effectively not able to participate in the land reform programme (Balmori 2003).

But most adverse impacts on gender are not as obvious as this. A number of tools for analysing budget proposals have therefore been developed with the aim of revealing the impacts of budget proposals on men and women (ibid.). These involve disaggregating public expenditure and government revenue or estimates of these and establishing how their effects are distributed in terms of benefits received or activity generated. For example, a government initiative or programme may apparently deliver financial or social benefits to women but without taking account of the fact that that programme relies heavily on the unpaid labour of the female members of a household to implement it. However, gender budget analysis is difficult to carry out if data do not exist or are unreliable.

Much of this gender budget analysis can be and is carried out within governments themselves as part of the process of preparing a budget. Governments may be mandated by law or by a government-adopted practice to undertake gender budget analysis. But civil society has played an important role in advocating for gender budget analysis and contributing to it as an independent actor in its own right or in collaboration with the government.

Members of Parliament individually have been advocates for gender budgeting initiatives, though as gender budgeting, to be effective, must be built into the preparation phase of the budget process, institutional legislative involvement is limited. However, legislatures can appraise budgets for their impact on gender if they choose to do so. Legislative involvement with gender budget initiatives has been particularly marked in South Africa. In 1995 the Women's Budget Initiative was established as a collaborative venture of two non-governmental organisations (NGOs) and the Gender and Economic Policy group of the Parliament's Finance Committee (Budlender 2001). The initiative eventually led to the analysis of all votes of the national budget and also expanded its reach into provincial and local government budget studies. One of the South African provinces, Gauteng, formalised this in 2003 by establishing a gender committee with powers to oversee the implementation of gender mainstreaming in the provisional government (Maseko 2006). The committee monitors policy commitments on gender development and equality for their translation into actual programmes with financial outputs committed to them. (However, this work has been hampered by lack of gender-disaggregated data.)

It has been emphasised that gender budgeting initiatives do not aim to produce a separate 'women's budget' (Balmori 2003, Maseko 2006). Rather, their aim is to incorporate awareness of gender into the process of formulating the country's budget in the first place. In this sense they aim to enlighten the decision-making process by revealing the implications of policy choices that might not otherwise be apparent. However, for their supporters, gender budget initiatives are also a means of advocating for budget policies that contribute to their wider social goals on equality. They therefore become part of the context in which alternative budget policies are debated and decided on.

Budget forecast constraints

Another institutional way in which a government's budget preparation capacity may be inhibited is by controlling directly the assumptions that governments make (as to economic growth, tax receipts, and so on) in taking budget decisions. Obviously, if a government's economic assumptions are too optimistic, the outcome of its budget policies will be less appropriate for the underlying economy than would otherwise be the case. Governments must always make assumptions or forecasts in preparing policies and sometimes these will simply be wrong or will be affected by entirely unpredictable events. Balanced budget legislation and similar policies usually make some allowance for wrong forecasting. But forecasting that is wholly in the government's own hands is inherently suspect. To minimise the risk of over-optimism on their part, governments can be constrained as to the forecasts on which they base their budget decisions.

Canada has done this since 1993. Experiences with overoptimistic economic assumptions being used in the budget had seriously undermined confidence in government economic forecasting. Consequently, in that year a policy was adopted of governments using an average of forecasts made by private sector economic forecasters in making budget decisions. These private sector forecasts are then, as a further measure of prudence, adjusted downwards by adding 0.5–1.0 percent to the average forecasts for interest rates and feeding this through the government's econometric model, thus producing lower forecast economic activity than even private sector economists are forecasting. To this buffer for meeting its fiscal objectives, the government adds a significant contingency reserve with restraints on its use (Blöndel 2001a).

These steps ensure that the assumptions that the government makes about the economic climate in which its budget is being prepared are conservative, thus counteracting any natural tendency on the part of government to assume better than likely outcomes. These conservative assumptions then form an institutional constraint on the preparation of the budget.

INVOLVEMENT IN PREPARING A BUDGET

How a government goes about preparing a budget is essentially a matter for it to decide. The preparation of a budget will necessarily be a bureaucratic exercise, involving extensive analysis, reporting, consultation, negotiation and decision-making within government. In this section it is proposed to consider some of the actual or potential contributions that can be made to budget preparation.

Ministers

Budget preparation is likely to be centralised even within government.

Not all ministers are equally involved in budget preparation. Indeed, the budget process can tip the political balance within a government, at least temporarily. Ministers of Finance are clearly central to budget preparation, while other ministers with little or no economic policy responsibilities may be only marginally involved. Even ministers with responsibility for large-spending departments may only be involved insofar as their departments' budget bids are concerned, without any ongoing or overall association with budget preparation. Often only the President or Prime Minister and the finance minister will be privy to the final form of the budget, with its full contents being disclosed to ministers shortly before it is announced to the legislature.

Ministerial arrangements for contributing to budget decisions can be formal or informal. For example, in Australia an Expenditure Review Committee is formed chaired by the Treasurer and comprised of the Prime Minister, the Deputy Prime Minister and the Minister of Finance. It receives submissions from departments for matters that they would like to see included in the budget. Other states may use Cabinet committees or ministerial groups to resolve policy issues as part of the process of preparing the budget. In the United Kingdom ministers have been reported as writing informally to the Chancellor of the Exchequer with proposals of matters that they would like to see included in the budget.[6]

Members of Parliament

There are examples of legislatures or legislative committees being formally involved in contributing to budget preparation at a strategic or macro level. These instances (Canada, Uganda and Sweden particularly) will be noted below when involvement in budget strategy is discussed. But at the basic initial level there is likely to be little, if any, involvement of Members of Parliament who hold no ministerial office in the preparation of the budget. Of course, the dynamics of party politics mean that backbench members of a party in government, in particular, have access to ministers and may exercise influence with them that is different from the access

---

6. For example, 'Brown snubs Miliband's idea for green taxes to save planet', *Sunday Telegraph*, 29 October 2006.

and influence that other members have and can exert. Party or 'caucus' committees may be established to contribute this input. Prime Ministers will be concerned to ensure that their backbench supporters feel involved with and committed to the policies that a government will espouse in its budget, and meetings of a formal and informal nature will be held to foster this. Ideas for inclusion of matters in the budget can emerge in this way. In practice, ministers may have greater difficulty persuading their own supporters of the value of proposed budget measures than they have in the legislature itself. But these consultations occur behind closed doors.

Within coalition governments there will need to be more extensive consultation and negotiation with Members of Parliament to ensure that cross-party agreement on important policy initiatives is maintained (especially on those policies not already defined in any existing coalition agreement). In minority government situations accommodations may need to be made with opposition parties ahead of the budget's finalisation. But these arrangements whereby political accommodations are reached between parties will operate outside the formal parliamentary structure and little information may be available about them.

While the contribution of individual Members of Parliament to budget preparation is not great (or is too difficult to identify), Parliamentarians are elected representatives and usually have strong roots in local communities. They can, at least potentially, be an effective means of communicating grassroots concerns that deserve to be taken into consideration in the making of a budget. Members can reflect these views by using parliamentary channels such as debates or questions or by using more informal links with ministers. Government spending in a member's constituency will often dominate that a member's contribution to budget preparation at the expense of strategic matters. This has been the subject of criticism as constituting too narrow or parochial an approach (Burnell 2001). But the adage that all politics is local is a reflection of the need not to allow a 'big picture' approach to ignore the impact of policy on the ground. Individual Members of Parliament in touch with constituency interests can provide this perspective. It may be that this has not been fully recognised in the past.

Legislative involvement

Direct legislative involvement in the budget preparation phase is uncommon. Legislatures generally lack the capacity to participate effectively in making a budget. Even in a legislative system with considerable budgetary capacity, such as the United States of America, the executive still takes the initiative in preparing and submitting a national budget. The legislature's budgetary capacity is then utilised in reviewing it (very extensively in that country). This suggests that lack of capacity is not the effective reason for lack of legislative involvement at the initiatory stage.

The major reason in most parliamentary systems why there is little legislative involvement in preparing the budget has already been remarked – that it is seen as an executive responsibility that is inextricably linked with the retention of office by the government. For an executive to surrender responsibility for preparing the budget to the legislature would be to abdicate its responsibility for governing. An ostensibly 'constitutional' impediment has thus been seen as precluding legislative involvement in the preparation phase of the budget process. (The issue of whether a budget in all its aspects actually does involve a question of confidence and whether amendment of a budget by the legislature in the subsequent, approval, phase of the budget process is possible, will be discussed later.) In essence, a budget is prepared by the executive without the participation of the legislature.

While there may be objections to the absolute exclusion of legislatures in this phase, it does have an important consequence. That is, that in a system where budget preparation is exclusively an executive task, responsibility for the measures being proposed is clear. There is no diffusion or occlusion of responsibility, as could be the case if different constitutional elements were participating in such decisions. The government is directly responsible for the budget proposals that it puts before the legislature. But whether the advantage of this clear line of responsibility and thus accountability also necessitates rigidly excluding all prior legislative participation in the preparation of a budget, is another question. (A similar issue arises in respect of legislative amendment of a budget.) A number of countries have found that it is possible for the legislature to play some role in budget preparation without compromising the identification of the executive's responsibility for it.

The major example of the latter occurs in Sweden where extensive discussions are held within the Parliament as part of the budget preparation phase. This leads to Parliament determining the overall level of public expenditure, though without allocating expenditures to particular sectors or programmes. The government itself carries out that allocation and presents a set of budget proposals consistent with the overall total approved by Parliament. This is legislative involvement in the preparation of a budget of the highest order. It has evolved in a country which has traditionally been consensual in its approach to politics, with coalition government a very common occurrence. In this way a national predisposition to inclusiveness may have been allied to political necessity.

Uganda has recently defined in law a process for interaction between the government and the Parliament in budget preparation. While this law was introduced under a single-party system, it has survived into the multi-party system that has replaced it.

In Uganda a budget framework paper must be submitted to Parliament following extensive consultations with civil society. The Parliament then has three to four weeks to give its views on the framework. The procedure Parliament follows is to refer the framework to its budget and finance committees for consideration and then to resolve on its position in the light of the committees' reports. Experience with this process so far suggests that members have difficulty distinguishing between strategic issues and questions of local funding of projects. Relatively few parliamentary suggestions have found their way into the subsequent budget. However, as experience of this process grows, and with the support of Uganda's

Parliamentary Budget Office, it can be expected that the legislature will become a more significant influence on budget preparation in the future.

Canada too has had a formal process of involving the House of Commons in the budget preparation phase. In 1994 this began to take the form of hearings by the Finance Committee on an economic and fiscal update that is presented some months ahead of the budget. The committee holds public hearings on the update and makes recommendations directed to the government for the inclusion of matters in the budget. The committee process has even been described as being held 'on behalf of' the Minister of Finance (Malloy 2006). While it is difficult to say how influential these hearings have been on the form of the final budget, they have become an accepted and valued part of the budget preparation phase (ibid.). In South Africa a means of legislative involvement in the budget preparation phase was suggested by the executive itself. The National Treasury, in a series of guidelines it developed in 2005, has proposed that portfolio committees in reporting on departmental annual reports should do so in time for the committees' views to be taken into account in making the next budget allocations (National Treasury, South Africa 2005).

These legislative practices amount to non-ministerial Parliamentarians having some formal input into a budget. In Sweden's case the input is considerable at the macro level (indeed, this involvement continues at a more detailed level during the phase of approving the budget). In the other cases the input is still more marginal. Despite this, the practice of opening up committee hearings for pre-budget submissions does help to channel input to the budget from the wider public through the legislature. This role of legislatures as a means of injecting an element of public opinion into the formulation of the budget has been distinctly under-realised to date. It would seem that this is an area in which legislatures could take the initiative to improve their own and the public's participation in the budget preparation phase.

Civil society's involvement

Anyone can advocate for the inclusion of particular measures in a budget without waiting to be invited to do so. The fact that a budget is an annual event in every country's public life is known. Individuals and groups can prepare proposals in time for it. Advocacy of budget measures can take the form of a direct communication to the government of one's views, using media outlets, protests or other forms of publicity. This is no different from the process followed by any person or group who wishes to advance a particular point of view and change public policy.

However, the regularity and the central importance of the budget have meant that contributions from civil society to a government's thinking during the budget preparation phase can be recognised and given in a more organised form. Governments may invite or encourage submissions at both a pre-budget and a final budget preparation stage.

Thus in Malaysia, the Treasury holds a budget dialogue. This involves the convening of meetings with the private sector, economists, research organisations, industrialists, trade and professional associations and non-governmental organisations, to solicit their views on the forthcoming budget. The legislature is not involved in this dialogue. In Uganda the budget law mandates national consultation on the budget as part of budget preparation. The government must produce a medium-term expenditure framework. Sector groups and local government can then contribute their views on budget strategies and priorities in the light of this framework. Ministers must consider these inputs as part of devising national and sector budget papers that are submitted to the legislature in advance of the budget proper. Occasionally, this contribution to budget preparation from civil society can be made or partially made through parliamentary hearings. This occurs in Canada in hearings on the government's economic and fiscal update.

In most countries civil society is at liberty to make proposals to the government for the inclusion of policies in the budget and governments will give consideration to them. These contributions are part of the ongoing operation of democracy and augment the information and views available to governments in framing economic and fiscal policy.

Generally, civil society's involvement in the preparation of a budget has been seen in terms of the submissions that it makes directly to the government in an endeavour to influence the government's budget decisions. However, as was remarked in the previous section on legislative involvement, there would seem to be much scope for this involvement to be channelled through the legislature as the representative; indeed, in a political sense the embodiment, of civil society. It is not unreasonable to claim this position for legislatures which, after all, enjoy the legitimacy of having members who have been elected to office by civil society. There would thus seem to be a largely untapped opportunity for legislatures to interact with civil society directly over budget proposals and transmit these to government (if concurred in by members) with the imprimatur of an elected body.

Participatory budgeting

The idea of civil society's involvement in the budget process has been taken a stage further in a policy-making process known as participatory budgeting. In this process citizens are not restricted to expressing their views about the contents of the budget; they are involved in making budget decisions themselves. So far participatory budgeting has been confined to the sub-national level in a number of states and municipalities in Brazil (though it is understood that further experiments in participatory budgeting are under way in Argentina and South Africa).

Participatory budgeting was first introduced in a Brazilian municipality in 1989. By June 2000 nearly 100 municipalities and five states had implemented some form of participatory budgeting programme. In one municipality alone in 1992 over 20,000 people participated in the programme (Wampler 2000 – from which the summary in this section is drawn). The programme is intended as a means of helping poorer citizens and neighbourhoods to receive better information about, and have control over greater levels of, public spending than would otherwise be the case. It is explicitly redistributive between localities in its aims with proportionately greater budgetary allocations being made to poorer localities.

Participatory budgeting involves the executive handing over to local people decision-making power on policy outcomes. It necessitates discretionary funding being set aside on a local basis for policy allocation. In the municipalities that are operating successful programmes this tends to represent 12–15 percent of their total budgets. While principally focused on spending decisions, meetings of participating citizens find that they are also drawn into discussing the overall financial health of the municipality, with generalised discussions on taxation and collection rates leading to efforts to improve the latter that involve the community.

The process followed usually involves the executive disseminating budgetary information and organising neighbourhood meetings. These neighbourhood meetings hold initial policy discussions and appoint representatives to regional meetings. The number of representatives each neighbourhood appoints to such meetings depends upon the level of participation in its own meeting.

Meetings (neighbourhood and regional) tend to be roughly two hours in duration with speakers limited to making short contributions. The first part of each meeting is concerned with exchanging information. The meetings then take the form of question-and-answer discussions on potential policies.

Most participatory budgeting decisions are directed to specific public works projects (for example, street paving, housing, clinics or small hospitals). In this way the decision-making process within the limits of the spending allocated to each locality is decentralised and communities are given a measure of control over their own development. However, where participatory budgeting has been operating for some time a gravitation to discussions of more general social policies has been remarked. Through participatory budgeting citizens have come to play a role in establishing the general priorities of the municipalities they inhabit, thus broadening their democratic base and fostering social solidarity. Greater citizen involvement in municipal decision-making is also claimed to counteract bureaucratic inefficiencies and corruption as citizens become better informed and demand greater efficiency and honesty in municipal administration. In support of citizen involvement, NGOs and other citizens' groups have taken to contributing newsletters and information on municipal affairs.

Participatory budgeting is still in its infancy and cautionary observations about it have been made.

It relies principally on executive initiative. Groups tend to focus on the executive's proposals rather than devising their own. As some form of organisation is necessary to start the programme and maintain it, this is more likely to be the case than not. In this way participatory budgeting has been seen as being to some extent a process of legitimising the executive's policy choices rather than enabling a real grassroots policy freedom to be exercised. There is also a danger of capture by well-informed activists who are able to organise and dominate the meetings, though it is hoped that this is only an initial problem. Once participatory budgeting has been operating for some time it is expected that the general political knowledge of the community will increase and tend to counteract activist influence. It is the case too that those advocating greater gender awareness in the formulation of budgets have found that participatory budgeting is not necessarily a gender-sensitive process. In some instances women's participation in planning activities, budget formulation and oversight activities has posed challenges similar to those arising in other forms of political participation where the traditional players are male (Balmori 2003).

In a study primarily directed to the legislature's role in the budget process it is also necessary to ask, what is the legislature's involvement in participatory budgeting? In fact, it seems to have little or none as an institution, though individual legislators may attend and participate in neighbourhood meetings. Indeed, the object of participatory budgeting is to enable citizens, not legislators, to make policy decisions. That participatory budgeting has to date developed principally in Brazil has been seen to be connected with the relatively weak role of legislatures (at various levels) in that country. To some extent participatory budgeting as it has operated hitherto appears to have bypassed legislatures.

Participatory budgeting has not yet been implemented at a national level and clearly there would be major logistical problems in doing so. However, it has operated in states and municipalities with up to 2 million inhabitants (Wampler 2000). This suggests that it may well be practicable in smaller nation states.

BUDGET STRATEGY

Budgeting is an annual event but it is an event that contributes to the realisation of a strategy or goals that have a more longer-term operation than one year. How budgeting relates to more long-term strategies than the current year must therefore be considered. But even in respect of the contents of a particular year's budget, part of its preparation phase is likely to be concerned with devising a strategy for the framing of *that* budget and revealing what that strategy is. Finally, and also as part of strategic input to budget-making, economic and fiscal information and forecasts may be required so as to establish the economic context in which budget decisions are to be taken.

One internationally recognised long-term strategy is the Millennium Development Goals (MDGs). These were developed following the United Nations Millennium Summit held in September 2000. The MDGs comprise a framework of eight goals, 18 international development targets and 48 indicators. These are designed to lead towards the eradication of poverty, the promotion of education, the equality of women and the improvement of health and the environment. The aim is to achieve sustainable development levels by 2015. The adoption of the goals has been followed up by a compact between developed and developing countries recognising mutual responsibilities for promoting the MDGs. The achievement of the goals is co-ordinated and monitored by the United Nations Development Programme which produces regular reports on progress.

A number of countries have devised their own long-term strategies for economic development. Trinidad and Tobago, for example, has adopted a strategy known as 'Vision 2020'. The aim of this strategy, and therefore the theme of budgets produced as part of it, is to use the revenue currently being obtained from that country's energy resources to develop a diversified and internationally competitive *non-energy* economy.

Uganda has adopted a particularly elaborate national planning strategy to guide public action (including in budget-making) to promote economic growth and eradicate absolute poverty. This is known as the Poverty Eradication Action Plan (PEAP). It was first adopted in 1997, and revised in 2000 and again in 2004. The current PEAP is intended to run through to 2008. It establishes five 'pillars' reflecting specific outcomes: (1) economic management; (2) enhancing production, competitiveness and incomes; (3) security, conflict resolution and disaster management; (4) good governance, and (5) human development. Specific objectives are outlined designed to lead to accomplishment of the pillars.

Such high-level strategies (which are broader in subject content than even a budget) thus inform and control the preparation of budgets over a period. They provide an overarching guide to governments in testing proposed budget measures. They also provide observers with benchmarks to judge whether a particular budget contributes to the long-term strategy expressed in them. Provided that the strategies are sound (and they will need revision periodically, as in the case of Uganda's PEAP) they may be seen as benign, even beneficial, constraints on budget-making.

Apart from the adoption of a long-term strategy such as the MDGs to which individual budgets contribute, there is some acknowledgement that it is desirable to have a longer-term budget framework than simply one year. The World Bank has encouraged governments to develop multi-year or medium-term expenditure frameworks that allow legislatures to look at priorities on a rolling basis, rather than viewing the budget as a single event (Regional Seminar for Parliaments of South-West Africa 2003). In the Netherlands governments are expected to establish an explicit overall budgetary policy for their term of office (as part of a coalition agreement). This overall budgetary policy is then translated into operational terms in the annual budgets. Other countries (such as Uganda) have adopted or experimented with 'rolling' budgets over a future period such as three years, that give an indication of expenditure patterns over the medium term, though in most cases these do not take the form of legal commitments or approvals and so do not require legislative endorsement. Associated with this is the practice of publishing economic and fiscal forecasts for an extended period ahead, usually taking a 'medium-term' view of economic prospects that will influence budget-making. In South Africa, for example, legislation requires that such projections be made.

In Tanzania a gender budget initiative has taken this a step further by attempting to build a gender perspective into the economic model used to develop the medium-term economic framework. An NGO in collaboration with the Ministry of Finance has developed a checklist for planners and budget officers to help them include gender considerations in the medium-term budget strategy. The checklist addresses how policy initiatives and programmes are developed and illustrates their effects on gender and gender relations (Balmori 2003).

Apart from these longer-term or multi-year projections, governments are increasingly disclosing the strategy that they intend to follow in preparing their next budget through budget strategy or pre-budget reports.

In many cases these reports take the form of economic and fiscal information and forecasts that describe the economic context within which the budget is being prepared and relate possible budget policies to the resources necessary to achieve them, rather than disclosing the actual measures to be included in the budget. Thus in South Africa legislation requires that pre-budget statements be released no later than one month before the presentation of the budget. The statements must discuss the macro-economic outlook, the fiscal framework for the budget and the main spending policy parameters. They set out the strategy which budget decisions are intended to realise (though budget plans themselves still need to be developed taking account of the overall availability of resources). This is part of the interaction between strategic planning and budgeting (Mwale 2005). The Canadian practice of issuing an economic and fiscal update has already been described. The set of economic data that is published as part of this update leads to a parliamentary committee hearing that may contribute to the preparation of the budget.

As well as pre-budget reporting that discloses economic and fiscal information, there are a number of instances where disclosure goes further than this and extends to a description of the government's policy intentions for the forthcoming budget either at a strategic level or in respect of particular policies under consideration for inclusion in the budget. This is a major change in approach from the absolute secrecy that has traditionally surrounded anything being considered as a budget measure. (This is discussed further below.)

The OECD has recommended that a pre-budget report should be released no later than one month before the budget is introduced. In the OECD's view this should state explicitly the government's long-term economic and fiscal policy objectives and economic and fiscal policy intentions for the forthcoming budget (and the two after that (Blöndel 2001b). A pre-budget report is released by the United Kingdom government several months before the budget. This report updates economic and public finance forecasts but it also describes new policies being considered by the government. A budget strategy report must be presented in New Zealand some months before the budget is delivered. Committee hearings are held on these reports.

In Uganda the budget law requires the presentation to Parliament of a budget strategy document. This document is formulated after national consultation on the budget with civil society (described above). Ministers consider the outcomes of this consultation and draw up a national budget framework paper and sector budget framework papers. These documents are submitted to Parliament and considered by the budget and finance committees. Parliament has an opportunity to decide on its view regarding the plans revealed in these frameworks. The budget is presented some time after Parliament's expression of its views on the budget strategy, though the latter is not binding on the government.

Thus, increasingly, information is being made available in the preparation phase of the budget process that describes the context in which the budget is being prepared, identifies its goals or even foreshadows its actual contents. This enables the government's forecasts and intentions to be subjected to analysis both by legislatures and by the public generally. In Uganda the Parliamentary Budget Office examines the pre-budget material, reports on it, and assists parliamentary committees and members to appraise it. Committee hearings may be held in legislatures on pre-budget reports and these may contribute to the formulation of policy for eventual inclusion in the budget. But legislative endorsement of a budget strategy (except in the sense of Sweden's approval of macro-level expenditure) is not generally required. Pre-budget disclosure obligations (where they exist) require disclosure of forecasts, information and intentions. They do not require the government to seek the approval of the legislature to proceed as announced, and there is little evidence that major changes in budgetary policy result from them. They do, however, serve the purpose of clarifying and making transparent a government's likely direction in its budget measures.

The matters discussed above relate to the disclosure of forecast information and budget strategy in advance of the delivery of the budget itself. But there may be, either in addition or instead, an obligation to present information and forecasts or to explain budget strategy at the time of the budget's delivery. As these latter are not made public prior to the budget, they do not enter into public debate and contribute to budget preparation from an external perspective. Nevertheless, the preparation of such material will have been proceeding within the executive in tandem with budget preparation and will contribute to the construction of the budget, both as data that influence and control the decisions that are taken and as the strategy guiding the government. This material is examined below when the presentation of the budget is discussed.

BUDGET SECRECY

Traditionally secrecy has surrounded the preparation of a budget up to the time of its presentation to the legislature. In 1948 a British Chancellor of the Exchequer who disclosed the contents of his budget to a journalist on his way into the House of Commons to deliver it, felt constrained to resign as a result even though the information did not appear in print until after the budget had been delivered and no person benefited or was disadvantaged as a result. So strongly was the convention of budget secrecy felt to operate, that Chancellors did not make public speeches for weeks before a budget was to be delivered in case they inadvertently revealed what budget measures were in contemplation. They were said to be 'in purdah' during this period.

As will be apparent from this, there are two aspects to the secrecy that has been held to apply to a budget. The first is in the preparation stage and relates to matters under consideration at that stage. The second relates to the announcement of the budget's contents itself.

To take the second aspect first. Secrecy has been said to be necessary so that no one can profit by trading on information as to a budget's contents before these are publicly available. In the corporate sector there is a parallel with insider trading. Information available to one person should be available to all. It is in regard to tax changes that this danger is particularly acute, but foreknowledge of other budget measures with identifiable financial consequences is also unacceptable. However, not all budget measures are of this nature and an assessment of the application of secrecy according to what is sensitive and what is not, might lead one to the conclusion that, while parts of a budget must be kept secret, other parts need not be. But this has not been the understanding of the convention. In the United Kingdom the budget has historically been identified with the announcement of tax changes. It is understandable how a convention of budget secrecy grew up in this context. But this does not explain why other countries have applied this convention of secrecy in budget contexts that were never wholly concerned with taxation or even with financially sensitive measures.

The real reason for secrecy as to a budget's contents would seem to stem from the budget being (in one sense) an *event*. As already remarked, it is the pre-eminent annual parliamentary occasion on which a government's most important economic and fiscal measures are announced. If those measures were publicly made known on an ad hoc basis before the delivery of the budget, there would be no event to celebrate and the budget as an event would cease to be significant. While it may be a trite reason, the budget's survival as an institution depends upon a degree of secrecy applying to its contents.

However, the decision as to what to include in a budget is essentially one for the government to make. Thus in New Zealand in 2006 the premature leak of a government decision on regulating access to broadband services intended to be announced in the budget, led the government to bring that announcement forward for release ahead of the budget. There was no necessity for such a decision to be reserved for announcement in the budget, though having been taken by the government in close proximity to budget day it had been scheduled for inclusion in it. But this was purely adventitious. Since a government determines the contents of a budget (though there may be strong expectations, for example, concerning tax measures, about what a budget will contain), it is always the government that determines what is to be included in it and therefore what is to be regarded as secret.

This is not wholly satisfactory. At the very least it brings into question why a 'budget leak' should be regarded as in all circumstances a serious matter. (Where someone stands to gain financially from such a leak it clearly is a serious matter.) If the application of secrecy or no secrecy is entirely determined by the government's decision as to whether to include the matter for announcement in its budget, it may be that a more relaxed view generally of the degree of confidentiality applying to budget announcements should be taken.

The other aspect of budget secrecy is secrecy in the course of a budget's preparation as to the measures that are in contemplation. Here it has been recognised that any such convention of secrecy has often been overstated by governments in order to discourage or prevent the involvement of others in the budget's preparation. This is not an acceptable reason for budget secrecy. As with the premature announcement of a budget's contents there could be circumstances in which the announcement that a particular measure was in contemplation would be undesirable for the speculation that it might encourage (for example, in a time of fixed exchange rates, that a devaluation was being considered). It is certainly the case that the disclosure of pre-budget material on a limited basis is unacceptable for the same reason that it would be improper for any person to receive information that might be financially valuable to them when that information is not available to all.

But there has been an increasing acknowledgement that budget preparation should be a more open process than a convention of absolute secrecy would permit and that the need for secrecy in this phase has been greatly overstated, particularly by governments. The developments already noted on the disclosure of fiscal information and forecasts and, even more, on the disclosure of budget strategies and possible budget measures mean that no such absolute rule can still apply. In Canada in 1994 pre-budget scrutiny was introduced, in part at least, to reduce this tradition of budget secrecy.

A further factor in regard to budget secrecy is the application of freedom of information legislation to information held as part of the budget process. A major reason for countries moving to introduce greater freedom of official information is to promote effective public participation in decision-making. Any convention of budget secrecy needs to be reassessed in the light of such a value. It is hardly consistent with it to suppress all information held by the government as part of the budget process until all decisions have been made. This is not to say that freedom of information principles render budget secrecy obsolete. Secrecy for budget information cannot have any validity beyond the delivery of the budget itself (though a longer budget cycle, such as a three-year period, may extend this in some circumstances). Thus budget secrecy has a limited life in any case. But within this time governments are entitled to some scope to consider issues out of the public eye. Better decision-making may arguably result if it is taken in the less pressured environment that may result.

Freedom of information principles thus demand a reassessment of the status of budget information in the preparation phase (though not necessarily total availability), particularly where the legislature has also made provision for public participation in that phase by requiring pre-budget reporting. Only if there is some relaxation in budget secrecy can such participation be fully informed and effective. While freedom of information legislation may not have entirely eliminated budget secrecy during the preparation of a budget, it has altered the balance in accordance with which the assessment of access to such information must be made.

Finally, it should be noted that one apparent exception to the principle of budget secrecy is the practice of having a 'lock-up' whereby journalists and others have the budget's contents disclosed to them in advance of the budget's delivery. Steps are normally taken to isolate those persons participating in the lock-up to ensure that they are not able to communicate with the outside world during this time. As well as the budget's contents being communicated to them, the finance minister or other ministers or officials may also brief the persons in the lock-up and elucidate the budget's provisions. In this way journalists are able to provide reporting and analysis of a budget as soon as its delivery is concluded, rather than having to spend several hours after it is delivered mastering its contents.

Because of the onerous conditions attached to a lock-up it is a release under an enforced embargo and is not a breach of budget secrecy.

3
Approval of the budget – the setting

BUDGET APPROVAL PHASE

While the preparation of a budget is essentially an executive function, the approval of a budget is almost exclusively a legislative one. It will be necessary to look below at exactly what is meant by 'approving a budget' because this differs depending upon each country's constitutional or procedural arrangements. But essentially budget approval transforms a set of proposals into a set of legal authorities, whether these relate to taxing or spending. Legal authority, of course, flows from the legislature; it is a prime function of any legislative body to confer this. Some legal authorities may be ongoing and so not need express legislative endorsement each year. Thus a tax, once imposed, may continue to operate and not require further legislative approval unless it is decided, as part of the budget, to alter its incidence or application. Conversely, a tax or a tax rate may require express legislative confirmation on an annual basis. Similarly, authorities to spend money, while in principle usually conferred on an annual basis (thus necessitating an annual budget), may be given a longer period of effect than one year or even applied for an indefinite time so that they do not require to be renewed annually by the legislature.

Traditionally, expenditures of high constitutional significance have been accorded this permanence. Thus judges' salaries have been permanent charges on public spending since the early eighteenth century to guarantee judges independence from financial pressure from the government or the legislature. However, too great a growth of such permanent authorities would undermine the legislature's annual role in budget approval. Proposals to confer it therefore need to be critically examined to see if they are appropriate. At the same time, it is necessary to ensure that expenditures under permanent authorities are included in accounts and other financial information presented to the legislature so that the total picture of spending (annual, longer-term or permanent) is revealed.

PRESENTATION OF THE BUDGET

Universally, budgets are presented to the legislature, though the responsibility for delivering the budget speech may lie with a President, a Prime Minister or a finance minister.

The maintenance of the legislature's central constitutional position makes it absolutely critical that major political developments take place there – and what more major political development is there than the delivery of the budget? Having a particular occasion on which budget measures are announced concentrates attention on parliamentary activity that may not otherwise be generated. It is also an acknowledgement of the legislature's central role in the next phase of the budget process, that in which the budget is approved.

The presentation of a government's comprehensive budget proposals to the legislature marks the end of the preparation phase of the budget process and the commencement of the approval phase: 'The executive's explanation to the legislature of its intentions for the next fiscal period is, so to speak, the climax of the whole preparatory stage of the budgetary process' (Knight and Wiltshire 1977). The point at which a budget is revealed in a speech or statement to the legislature is the focal point of the entire process. It is also the major occasion of the year in terms of the announcement of economic policy by the government and is predictably the main event in a legislature's annual transaction of business (though other, less predictable, dramatic and important events may occur in the course of the parliamentary year too).

Time of presentation

The presentation of a budget is an annual event whose timing has generally been left to the government to determine. The question arises as to what, apart from political calculation, is relevant in determining at what point in the year a budget should be presented? This in turn depends upon what is the country's fiscal or financial year.

The OECD, in recommending best practice for budget transparency, has suggested that a government's budget should be submitted at least three months prior to the start of the country's fiscal year. It also recommends that the parliamentary approval process of a budget should be completed by the start of the fiscal year so that an approved budget is in place once the year commences (Regional Seminar for Parliaments of South-West Africa 2003). The time by which a budget must be *approved* will be considered further below. However, in respect of those parliamentary systems where there is a high expectation that a government's budget will be endorsed without any significant amendment, the critical question is the date of its *presentation* rather than that of its eventual formal approval. In such countries budget transparency is served by the presentation of the budget. From that point on, conduct can proceed on the basis of the proposals set forth in the budget (the budget as prepared is seen as an authoritative decision in itself). In countries where the outcome of the budget approval process is less assured, of course, this is not the case and the time of that approval becomes more significant.

A number of countries, either as a matter of law or practice, do require that a budget is presented before the fiscal year commences. For example, the Indian Constitution requires that the budget be presented before the opening of the fiscal year. One problem with presenting a budget before the commencement of the fiscal year is that the previous year is still running and the financial outcomes of that year cannot be precisely known.

This is certainly a complicating factor but it should not be an insuperable obstacle to presenting a budget before the year opens and indeed has not been found to be so in those states that follow this practice. Provided that the budget is not presented too long before the end of the previous fiscal year a projection can be made of likely outturns and this projection made the basis of budget calculations. In any event, to wait for the outturns of the previous year to become available would inevitably lead to considerable delay in the budget approval phase, for final figures may not be available for some time (and even longer if audited figures are to be used). This would prolong the period during which interim finance authorities would be required to be obtained by the government and, as these authorities tend to be aggregated approvals, would not be conducive to transparency in regard to a government's financial authority (this is discussed further below).

While the question of not knowing precisely about outturns ought not to prevent a budget being presented before the fiscal year commences, many countries permit budgets to be presented during the course of the year to which they relate. In Trinidad and Tobago and New Zealand, for instance, a budget must be presented within one month of the opening of the fiscal year, though the government may, in practice, choose to present it much earlier than this if it wishes. In New Zealand's case, indeed, the practice is to present the budget some six weeks before the commencement of the fiscal year. In both of these countries, political practice is such that it can be assumed that the budget will be passed by the legislature in the form that it is presented. Thus the budget's delivery to the legislature is a strongly reliable indication of budgetary outcomes.

In countries where the outcome of the budget approval process is more problematic or where presentation of the budget is delayed until much later in the fiscal year to which it relates, the position is less satisfactory. The late presentation of a budget in Zambia, for instance, has been criticised on these grounds (Burnell 2001).

Manner of presentation

The heart of the entire budget process is the delivery of a speech or statement to the legislature setting out the government's budget proposals. The presentation of the other supporting information already discussed, either on the same occasion or slightly later, does not attract the same attention.

A budget's delivery is an intensely political occasion. It is not just the technical delivery of a financial address. It is therefore natural that a government and particularly the minister delivering it will be at pains to put the proposals in the best possible light and emphasise its political appeal. There are few formal constraints on what may be in the statement. It is the government's statement and it is for the government to decide how to deliver it and what to include in it. One innovatory approach adopted in St Lucia, for example, was for the minister to use PowerPoint to illustrate the points he was making in his speech (Roberts 1999).

A budget speech may be very wide-ranging in its contents including in reviewing the year just ended or about to end. Two observers commenting in 1977 on Australian Treasurers' budget speeches thought that they sounded more like a combination of weather preview, crop forecast and shopping list rather than a sophisticated economic statement (Knight and Wiltshire 1977). Speeches differ in length from the relatively short to several hours depending upon the inclination of the minister and the rules of the assembly. But they are always liable to be intensely political.

BUDGET EXPLANATIONS

While budget preparation may be regarded as an event – the delivery of a speech or statement – it is today rarely confined to a single statement that can be reproduced as 'the budget'. Information supplementing the necessarily broad outline of the budgetary proposals that can be given in a speech, is an essential aspect of budget presentation. Such information provides the context within which the policies being announced are promoted, provides forecast information on their likely effects, and supplements and provides important details about them. Providing detailed information on budget decisions increases transparency in budgeting and is an essential element in public accountability. Presentation of a budget then, is much more than merely the delivery of a speech or statement by the finance minister.

Disclosure of the strategy that is to guide a government in the preparation of its budget at the preparatory stage has already been discussed along with pre-budget reporting. However, a budget strategy document may be presented at the time of presentation of the budget, as part of the budget documentation that is associated with the budget. Thus in India legislation enjoins the presentation of a number of strategy documents – on fiscal policy and other policy priorities – *along with* the budget. These documents do not set the strategic scene in advance of the budget as do pre-budget strategic documents. What they do is describe the strategy that the budget itself as announced to the legislature is intended to effect. They constitute a high-level comment on the measures rather than a prefiguring of them. Such information helps to explain what the government is attempting to achieve. Its policies can be judged against the goals of that strategy.

This requirement that the government explain what its 'plan' is for spending and taxation and what impact it expects that the measures it has announced will have is coming to be seen as an essential discipline on governments. While such reports are often presented at the same time as the budget is delivered, they may also follow soon afterwards.

As well as these questions as to the strategy or plan which the budget is intended to effect, budget law may require explanations of possible policy outcomes from other perspectives. In a number of countries the gender implications of budget proposals must be addressed in the supporting documentation. Thus gender budget statements may be presented as reports by the government on budget expenditure forecasts, relating these to how they affect gender equity objectives. They usually contain a gender budget analysis identifying gender biases in allocations, focusing on employment balances, shares of public expenditure and the effectiveness of targeted expenditure (Balmori 2003). The environmental effects of a policy or the effects on other groups which also have been disadvantaged historically and which are identified on an ethnic, regional or age basis, may be required to be specifically addressed in budget reporting.

For any of these reasons, budget law may require the government to report specifically on the possible outcomes of its policies. But this is a dynamic process. The need to report publicly on these factors is likely to prompt greater consideration of each policy's impact on these grounds in the first place. It may even prompt changes in the policy that negate adverse consequences that would have otherwise been required to be admitted to in the report. Indeed, this is often the aim of such requirements. They are not just a form of audit. They are intended to ensure that factors and groups that may have been otherwise overlooked or minimised in the policy-making process are recognised and accorded proper consideration, so leading to possible changes to the policy as adopted.

A budget, even as an event, is then a complicated process including other high-level strategic and planning documents apart from the traditional statement and forecasts and other economic and fiscal information. Budget presentation will also include presenting the government's detailed spending plans for the public sector, often known as the estimates or demands for grants of the government. This information can run to many documents. In Canada, for instance, over 80 separate budget documents are presented to the legislature in association with the budget.

This complexity, even to the most informed observers of budgetary practice, is a problem for public appreciation of a process that is of critical importance to all citizens. One way of addressing this is to produce a simplified summary of budget measures that can make the overall budget more comprehensible. A number of countries do this. In India, for example, one of the budget documents is a publication called 'Budget at a Glance'. This shows in brief, receipts and disbursements together with broad details of the tax revenues and other government receipts, an outline breakdown of public expenditure, transfers to state and union territory governments, and the fiscal position of the central government.

It must be said, however, that a modern budget is inevitably exceedingly difficult to comprehend and the proliferation of supporting information can be intimidating and discourage efforts to come to grips with the budget. This is so even among Members of Parliament who have the formal function of determining whether to approve it. Commentators have found little evidence of the use of this supporting information by legislators in the course of their approval or general oversight duties (Sterck and Bouckaert 2006). Partly this is due to a disinclination on the part of members to invest what can be seen as a disproportionate amount of time in mastering a budget's intricacies. To some extent access to expert advice within the legislature itself can help members in understanding the budget and compensate for this problem. But the disinclination also results from the limited impact that even well-informed members think that they can have on a budget during its parliamentary consideration.

CONTENTS OF BUDGET PROPOSALS

Although the budget speech itself is relatively unconstrained as to its contents, this is not so in regard to the specific proposals presented in or in association with the budget. The most important of these is the government's detailed spending proposals, known as estimates of expenditure or demands for grants. Governments will present estimates on a sectoral, programme or departmental basis and these estimates will be the legal basis for public spending once they have been endorsed by the legislature. In India these demands are presented in two stages. A demand is presented along with the budget usually seeking a single spending authority for each demand, though sometimes more than one for larger ministries or departments. Some time later when outturns are known but before parliamentary discussion on the demands begins, a further document is presented giving more details of the proposed expenditures and of the actual expenditures in the previous year.

The form in which these proposals are drawn up is of great potential importance both to the legislature's consideration of the proposals and to the final legal authority that is granted, though, in practice, the legislature often leaves the settling of this form to the government. The structure of the estimates has changed with the consolidation of demands (or votes) into fewer headings. The motivating factor for this has been greater executive flexibility in the use of its spending authority. This is not necessarily a bad thing but it may have reduced the legislature's capacity to oversee the expenditure. At the very least the legislature's interest in financial oversight means that this factor needs to be considered in any contemplated changes to the form in which financial authority is sought from the legislature. Ideally, the legislature or its lead finance committee should be fully involved in considering any such changes before they are made.

Spending authorities or appropriations have traditionally sought approval to expend sums of money (cash appropriations) on such tangible things as personnel and equipment (inputs). These forms of authorities still predominate. However, increasingly, the focus of appropriating public money has shifted to what the money is intended to achieve (outputs) rather than concentrating on the instruments that will be used to achieve them. Thus appropriations have shown a trend towards being output-based (the advice or services to be produced) rather than input-based (the staff or equipment that will provide that advice or service). In a further development some countries are experimenting with going beyond outputs and attempting to define appropriations by the goals or objectives that those outputs are designed to contribute to. Advice and services are not ends in themselves. Hopefully they contribute to social goals such as the effective education and health systems which communities desire. These are often referred to as outcomes with an attempt being made to budget for them on an outcome basis. However, an attendant danger with output-based and outcome-based appropriations is that the terms in which they are expressed can be so general that they are effectively a grant of expenditure authority on a 'blank-cheque' basis.

As appropriations are moving to output or outcome bases they are no longer exclusively expressed in cash terms. They are coming to be expressed in terms of the costs, liabilities or expenses that will be incurred in current expenditure terms and (separately) the capital expenditure they will require. Accounting systems too are changing to reflect this non-cash basis for appropriating funds. Accounting on an accruals basis is replacing cash accounting. Under accruals accounting expenses are recognised in the public accounts when they are incurred rather than when payment for the goods and services purchased with that expense is made. Public entities produce balance sheets recording their assets and liabilities. The aims of these changes are to encourage more efficient use of public resources and to focus attention on the objectives of spending public money rather than on the fact of its legal availability to be expended.

One consequence of this emphasis on objectives is the need to devise means of measuring whether these objectives have been achieved. Thus it has become compulsory for departments and agencies to agree to performance targets or standards as part of the budget process. Provided that these are realistic and measurable it should be possible to establish how well the department or agency performed in utilising the spending authorities conferred on it. The remuneration of officials may be made to depend, at least in part, on meeting those targets. This is a matter to which we will return when financial oversight is considered.

Laudable as these developments are they undeniably make a complex process even more complex. Cash appropriations may be inadequate as a system but they are more comprehensible, at least to a financial layperson. This again emphasises the importance of legislative support in the budget process, not only in understanding the budget proposals that are put to it on an annual basis but so that legislatures can contribute to the developments going on in the appropriation system and ensure that the system adopted is as comprehensible as possible. The support available to legislatures is discussed in the next chapter.

THE FORM OF APPROVAL REQUIRED FOR A BUDGET

Thus far reference has been made to legislative approval of the executive's budget proposals. It is true that legislative approval is invariably required but this begs the question of what exactly is being approved and how that approval is signified. In the United Kingdom, for instance, approval of the 'budget' involves the House of Commons approving a number of tax resolutions immediately after the speech of the Chancellor of the Exchequer. These resolutions take effect in law on a temporary basis until given permanent effect later in the year in a finance bill. The expenditure side of the budget process is approved separately in legislation appropriating expenditure on a resource basis. In other jurisdictions approval of the budget may be given by the house agreeing to pass or give a second reading (in principle, approval) to a bill that embodies the budget's proposals. Because of the diverse nature of budget proposals there may not be a single bill embodying them. (In the Netherlands, for instance, the budget comprises 23 separate bills.) Nevertheless, a single bill or the stage of a single bill may conventionally be regarded as comprising the budget for approval purposes and the passage of that bill or the legislature's agreement to the passage of that stage may come to be regarded as approval of the budget. Technically, then, approval of the budget is signified by a distinct legislative decision that differs in detail depending upon each country's constitutional or legislative provisions.

In practice, it is not difficult to identify in each country what is the point at which the legislature's approval is given to the budget. This is important in any consideration of whether the survival of the government is in issue because the confidence of the legislature in the government is engaged when budget approval is involved. The approval of the detailed contents of a budget, such as the estimates, is considered as a separate part of the budget approval process. This too may involve further questions of confidence. It is necessary therefore to discuss briefly the concept of 'confidence'.

Approval of the budget will then be considered at three levels (the overall budget, its policy components, and individual appropriations), though not all levels may be present or may be specifically differentiated in every case.

Confidence of the legislature

The confidence of the legislature in the government means that a government can only continue to govern on the same basis as before if it can avoid defeat on a matter involving its survival in office or, alternatively, if it can demonstrate that it has the support of the legislature on such a matter. Thus a tied vote would not involve a loss of confidence in the former situation (the government would have avoided defeat) but it would in the latter since the government would have failed to demonstrate that it had the support of the House.

How confidence is defined and operates will differ from legislature to legislature and, perhaps, from issue to issue. For example, following a vote in the Italian Senate in February 2007 (not on a budget matter), the Italian government resigned despite winning the vote by 158 votes to 136. This was because there were 24 abstentions and abstentions were counted as votes against.[7]

The effect of a loss of a vote of confidence is a question to be determined by constitutional and political practice. In Canada in 1979 the defeat of the budget led to a general election. This is the most likely outcome. But an immediate election may be avoided if an alternative government can be formed from within the existing legislature. The alternative government that is formed in these circumstances may be led by the same Prime Minister and involve the same parties that were previously in office. However, the political mix must be different in some way (for example, another party may be brought into the coalition or an agreement made with a party outside the government for support of the budget) to justify

---

7. 'Pasta and fries', *The Economist*, 24 February 2007 (the government was subsequently confirmed in office).

the government being recommissioned in office once it has been defeated on something as important as its budget proposals.

Overall approval of a budget

The first level at which budget approval can be considered is the overall or macro level. This is high-level approval of a government's budget proposals, though the precise form of the proposition that the legislature is presented with in deciding whether or not to approve the budget will differ depending on the constitutional setting, relevant legislation and the legislature's own rules. It may be a resolution declaring agreement to the budget or the passing of a bill or bills or the legislature agreeing to a particular stage of a bill. Invariably, approval of the budget overall will involve a question of the confidence of the legislature in the government, though this will often be a matter of convention rather than a legal requirement.

A budget is not just something on which the government wishes to avoid defeat (though it clearly wishes to do that). It is something that a government positively has to persuade the legislature to pass. If a government could not get its budget passed it could not be considered to be governing.

If following defeat of a budget an alternative government is not practicable or if elections are due to be held soon in any case, an election may be called with the defeated government continuing in office in a caretaker capacity. For example, a caretaker government could, if necessary, present a 'neutral' budget to ensure the continued operation of government during the election period. Alternatively, the legislature may agree to give or extend interim budgetary authority to tide matters over for that period.

Budget approval, at least at this high level, is not just essential to the continuance of the government, it is an intrinsic aspect of governing. One goes with the other.

Approval of the components of a budget

The second level at which budget approval may be given is at the stage of individual approval for the several financial measures proposed in the budget. The budget speech is often a convenient means of announcing and linking together different policy proposals involving distinct sectors of the economy. Defeat or frustration of one of these policy proposals can be viewed differently from defeat of the budget as a whole. Not all budget proposals are of equal importance either economically or politically. Loss of one, while it would undoubtedly embarrass a government, need not be regarded sufficiently seriously to be treated as involving a matter of confidence. Of course, if a government itself elects to treat an individual policy as involving a matter of confidence, and declares that it will resign if that policy is not passed, it is perfectly entitled to do so (as in the Italian example given above). No government can be compelled to remain in office.

A threat from a government that it will resign if defeated on a part of its budget could be used by it to bring wavering supporters into line. The possibility of bringing down a government and putting another party into office or facing an early election may, in some members' minds, be more objectionable than the policy with which they disagree and they may consequently support the government though they dislike the policy. This is political brinkmanship on the part of a government. But, subject to the government putting itself at risk in this way, there does not appear to be any intrinsic reason why a government defeated on one aspect of its budget should automatically feel compelled to offer its resignation. Suggestions by the government that a budget defeat of this nature automatically involves a question of confidence may be motivated more by an attempt to gain support for its policies than out of a regard for constitutional propriety. Conversely, suggestions by the opposition that this automatically follows may be merely political opportunism. Whether defeat on an individual measure does involve a loss of confidence will always depend on the political significance of the budget rebuff the government has suffered rather than following as an automatic consequence.

Approval of individual appropriations

The third level to consider is the level of approval of individual appropriations (estimates).

The level at which and form in which appropriation proposals are put to the legislature itself differs depending upon the form of the estimates.

In principle, a failure to pass all appropriation proposals in the form presented by the government should not of itself demonstrate a loss of confidence in the government. But this proposition needs to be qualified. Defeat in a country whose political culture means that government defeat on the estimates is virtually unknown will inevitably assume more political significance than defeat in a country where this is commonplace. This does not mean that all defeats even in a country of the former type must lead to resignation. Australia is one country in which budget defeats are extremely rare. Yet in 1994 an amendment to reduce authorised capital expenditure in a particular appropriation was carried against the government, without bringing it down. But the threshold for treating such a defeat as involving loss of confidence would undoubtedly be lower in a country of that type.

On the other hand, even in a system in which the government's proposals are commonly changed, some expenditure proposals may be seen as fundamental and some legislative amendments of its proposals may individually or cumulatively be so significant or humiliating as to bring into question the government's ability or desire to remain in office. This will be a matter of political judgement depending upon the circumstances in that country at that time.

There is also the possibility that a legislature's rules may permit amendments to the estimates to be moved that explicitly or implicitly raise matters of confidence in the government. This may be expressed in the wording of the amendment that is moved, in reasons given for it, or in the form that it takes (for example, to reduce the salary of the Prime Minister). In such circumstances it may be difficult to escape the conclusion that a matter of confidence is involved. Finally, of course, as with individual budget proposals, governments may promote the idea that confidence is involved so as to maintain party unity.

Thus, while budget defeat at a detailed appropriation level can be regarded as less critical in a constitutional sense than defeat at a macro level, it cannot be entirely discounted as involving the confidence of the legislature in the government.

TIMING OF BUDGET APPROVAL

The timing of the budget's presentation to the legislature has been discussed above.[8] Closely related to rules on the time by which a budget must be presented are requirements (if any) by which that budget must receive legislative approval.

There is an initial conceptual difficulty with rules relating to the approval of a budget. That is, that the legislature may decide *not* to approve the budget or to defer approval indefinitely. As this is a political decision that is available, in theory anyway, to any legislature, there is no legal means of coercing legislative approval for a budget and nor should there be. If there were this would be a negation of democracy. Any rules requiring the legislature to approve a budget are therefore legally unenforceable, short of deeming a budget to be approved if a legislature has failed to pass it within a specified time. But this latter solution to legislative recalcitrance is usually reserved for the chamber of a legislature that has not been popularly elected. Thus the House of Lords has, since 1911, had only one month to consider money bills passed by the House of Commons. If the House of Lords has not passed such a bill at the end of that month, it may proceed to be enacted without that House's concurrence.

While this may be an acceptable means of limiting the powers of an unelected chamber and of resolving potential disputes between houses in a bicameral legislature, it is not acceptable as a general proposition as its adoption would dispense with legislative approval

---

8. See p. 37.

of a budget and substitute executive government for parliamentary government. It is necessary therefore to consider what is the fallback position if legislative approval is not obtained by a certain time. This is considered below.[9]

Given that budget approval rules cannot mean that the legislature is *obliged* to approve the budget by a certain time, do they have any utility? It would seem that they do – by giving consideration of the budget a priority in the parliamentary process that it might not otherwise receive. Such rules incentivise an executive to seek legislative endorsement by a certain time and to use its influence on the legislature's business programme to achieve this. Consideration of the budget does not just fall to the bottom of the legislative agenda. Budget approval rules also help to ensure that budget approval is given either before the fiscal year commences (a recommendation of the OECD) or shortly afterwards. An obvious advantage of seeking budget approval before the financial year opens is that if the budget is rejected the resulting political crisis (often involving an election) might be resolved before the opening of that year, thus avoiding any financial uncertainty. However, even with such a rule it may not be possible to resolve such a crisis in time. In most states, the prospect of budget rejection may be so remote anyway as to render such an advantage irrelevant.

Budget approval rules are in practice always aspirational, timetabling, rules, whether embodied in law (Uganda, two months after presentation) or in the legislature's own internal procedures (New Zealand, within three months of presentation).

LIMITATIONS ON THE NEED FOR LEGISLATIVE APPROVAL

While the requirement of legislative approval of a budget is universal there are limits or qualifications on this that require to be noted.

Firstly, the law (through legislation passed in an earlier year) may have made an ongoing provision for certain types of expenditure.

9. See p. 59 (reversionary budgets).

Permanent authorisations of this nature have been mentioned above.[10] This means that the annual budget presented to the legislature does not need to seek approval for expenditures already authorised in this way and the legislature's annual role in budget approval is relaxed (though authority for the permanently authorised expenditure still derives ultimately from the legislature). If a high proportion of total expenditure is permanently authorised in this way, this can seriously weaken the legislature's role in annual budget approval. Permanent authorisation of expenditure should therefore only be conceded if a compelling justification for it can be established. Indeed, it has been suggested that the ongoing justification for permanent appropriations should be kept under active review by linking these to 'sunset clauses' that would cause permanent appropriations to lapse if not renewed periodically (Kelly 2005). Even where permanent authorisation is justified, outturns of actual expenditure and estimates of future expenditure pursuant to those authorisations should still be placed before the legislature so that a total picture of annual expenditure is revealed. (While the term 'permanent' has been used in discussing this type of expenditure, 'indefinite' might be a better term for its appropriation status since it is always open to the legislature to repeal the legislation conferring the ongoing financial authorisation.)

Secondly, certain types of financial transactions may not require legislative approval because they are not expenditures. Grants received by the government, loans raised by it or other kinds of receipt may not of themselves require legislative approval yet they affect the public finances within which a government operates. Much of English parliamentary history involved the government (the Crown) attempting to escape parliamentary control by securing access to finance from non-parliamentary sources (which straightforward taxation was held to require). In Australia in 1975, a government explored alternative means (overseas loans) as a way of tiding it over while the Senate held up passage of budget legislation authorising expenditure.

10. See p. 35.

For this reason public finance legislation often converts the proceeds of a gift or a loan automatically into public money and provides that legislative authority is required for the expenditure or use of any public money. In these circumstances, the provenance of a government's funding is legally irrelevant (it may be economically significant). Its use still requires legislative approval.

Thirdly, departments or agencies may be given authority to carry forward funds previously appropriated to them and not expended at the time or to retain and use revenue generated in the course of their activities. Allowing finances to be operated on a revolving fund rather than a consolidated fund basis (whereby all surpluses and revenues are surrendered to a central government account) can remove the necessity to seek an annual appropriation from the legislature, thus freeing the entity from parliamentary control.

Finally, certain categories of expenditure may be put before the legislature in outline or in aggregate only and lack the specificity of other requests for legislative approval. Defence expenditure and expenditure on the security or intelligence services are examples of public spending that is often not fully disclosed even to the legislature that is asked to approve it. Defence expenditure may be an especially large proportion of a country's total spending, thus significantly reducing the legislature's effective role in the budget approval process. Instead, the legislature may be asked to approve a single aggregate total that discloses little or nothing about the uses to which such spending is to be put. In order to minimise the derogation of legislative control that such practices entail, committees may receive evidence on the expenditure in secret or leading legislators may receive confidential briefings on it.

PUBLIC-PRIVATE PARTNERSHIPS

New forms of institutional arrangement known as public-private partnerships (PPPs) also raise questions of a legislature's involvement in authorising public expenditure. PPPs have been employed in a number of different areas that would formerly have been developed solely by the public sector: infrastructural (building of roads, hospitals, houses, and so on) and operational (operating ports, prisons and toll roads, and so on) or a combination of these (for example, a public road built with private funds and a concession granted to the developer to charge a toll on the road for a number of years).

Though PPPs have attracted considerable attention in recent years it has been pointed out that there is nothing new in co-operation between the public and private sectors (Hodge and Greve 2007). Contracts to deliver, or to contribute towards the delivery of, public goods and services have existed for centuries. Despite this, the forms which these collaborations take have been developing in a number of ways and this is seen as justifying the recognition of PPPs as new organisational forms worth attention in their own right. But, as the plural expression suggests, there is no one form a PPP takes, nor is there an acceptable, comprehensive definition of what a PPP is. They have been said to differ from traditional contractual arrangements in being more long term, in sharing infrastructural decision-making, in generating bigger financial flows and, crucially, in sharing risks (ibid.).

There are major accountability issues associated with PPPs. These will be mentioned later as part of the discussion on evaluation of a budget.[11] But at this point it is worth remarking on the significance of PPPs as they enter into the budget-making process.

One of the reasons that has been identified for the increasing use of PPPs is as a means of reducing public sector debt and the consequent pressure on government budgets (ibid.; indeed, the authors discuss the view that PPPs are a means of, or a surrogate for, privatisation). It has been estimated that the United Kingdom raises some 15–20 percent of its capital budget each year through a particular PPP model it has developed known as the Private Finance Initiative, with the proportion as high as 50 percent in a sector such as transport (Pollitt 2005).

This private financing of public sector capital projects has been likened to a 'mega-credit card' available to governments and

11. See p. 106.

giving them the ability to initiate infrastructural developments with a minimum of delay (Hodge and Greve 2007). The extent to which the consequent lack of institutional control is an advantage (swifter implementation, drawing on private sector innovation, and so on) or a disadvantage (less rigorous costing of projects and alternatives, lack of overall control by government, and so on), is a controversial and unresolved issue. From a budget preparation point of view, however, the existence of PPPs making long-term financial commitments that may not be apparent in the annual budget documentation, poses challenges for legislatures.

An obvious issue is the extent to which a PPP effectively commits to public expenditure or at least the risk of public expenditure, without legislative endorsement in a budget. If PPPs are 'off-budget' financing arrangements, what prospective role does the legislature have in respect of them? It may be that the answer is: little or none.

Most of the literature on PPPs and their implications for legislatures, focuses on ex post facto accountability for the projects undertaken. This will be noted later. But an equally important issue may be finding an ex ante role for legislatures in examining or authorising the funding commitments for PPPs. The infinite variety that PPPs take militates against this. It could be that as a first step legislatures need to turn their attention to creating an overall consistency in the types of PPPs that may be entered into (the legislation applying to PPPs tends to be ad hoc) so that a means of budgetary legislative authorisation can be devised for this institutional form.

INTERIM APPROVALS

Where legislative approval is given to a budget before the fiscal year opens, expenditure authorisation is in place and a government can lawfully spend public money on its policies even though during the course of the year new policies or higher than expected spending may necessitate further or supplementary approvals from the legislature.

But many or even most budgets are not approved before the opening of the fiscal year. If spending authority is not to lapse at this time, provision must be made for interim authorisation to carry on government up to such time as budget approval is given.

Such an interim authority may be a standing authority to continue to spend public money in anticipation of budget approval. But such an open-ended authority risks turning an interim authority into a final one because it provides no incentive for a government to put detailed spending proposals before the legislature for endorsement if it can continue to spend indefinitely on an 'interim' basis. So where there is an automatic authority of this nature it may be limited to a few months of the new fiscal year or to a specified proportion (perhaps 25 percent) of authorised spending in the previous year. Before the interim authority runs out, the government will have to obtain legislative approval for its budget or otherwise get the legislature to renew or extend the interim spending authorisation.

Most countries will have some system requiring express legislative authorisation of interim spending ahead of budget approval. These are often known as 'votes on account'. In many countries such interim authorities are regularly required (for example, Malawi, the United Kingdom, Canada and India), while in others (for example, Malaysia), while recognised as possible, they are rarely used. An imminent election may render it necessary for a government to ask for interim authority if there is not time to pass a budget before the election or if it is not reasonable for a budget to be presented, for example, because the government has lost the confidence of the legislature.

The necessity to ask for interim authority means that a government has to account to the legislature at least as soon as the fiscal year opens. However, interim spending authorities do not usually contain the level of detail contained in a government's main expenditure proposals and can be accompanied by little or no economic and fiscal information. They often attract little parliamentary attention (by convention, in India they are treated as formal matters and are not discussed) or are considered in general debates which do not focus on the details of the proposed spending.

While legally necessary, interim authorisations are thus an unsatisfactory means of approving public expenditure for any lengthy period of time. Their use should be closely circumscribed.

SUBSEQUENT BUDGET APPROVALS

Typically the budget approval process is not complete on the legislature's agreement to the budget or to the detailed expenditure plans presented to it by the government. It is more than likely that these will need to be supplemented during the course of the fiscal year, as new policies are devised or the estimated expenditures on policies included in the budget are found to be wrong and require adjustment. Certainly, any change to the initial appropriations approved by the legislature will need legal sanction, though there is often authority for the government to transfer appropriations within limits (known as 'virement') between different classes of appropriation. Sometimes there may need to be more than one subsequent round in which additional or supplementary authority of this nature is sought.

A distinction is sometimes drawn between a supplementary *budget* which involves a change in the government's fiscal stance as compared to the main budget presented to the legislature, and supplementary *estimates* which are used to obtain authority for revised spending levels, including spending for contingencies. This distinction is observed in Canada, for example. But not all countries draw such a distinction and supplementary estimates can disguise important changes in the fiscal position made during the course of the fiscal year. Concern has been expressed that supplementary budgets can involve substantial expenditure increases as compared with the original budgetary proposals and that these are not necessarily made self-financing or offset against the provision for contingencies made in the main budget (IMF 2001).

These points emphasise the significance or potential significance of subsequent budget approval procedures. Indeed, in some countries the supplementary budget is regarded as the really important budget in economic and fiscal terms. Despite this, it is clear that legislatures and the public generally pay much less attention to supplementary budget and supplementary estimates than they do to the main budget and estimates. There is thus a suspicion that supplementary approvals have been used to fund a number of important political initiatives attracting the consequently weaker parliamentary oversight of the supplementary budget process (Dobell and Ulrich 2006).

In Canada, the practice is that the funding for new policies announced in the budget that still require legislative approval is not included in the estimates presented with the budget. Such funding is included in supplementary estimates once parliamentary approval of those policies has been given. This makes the extra funding for policies that are legally contingent quite explicit, though this is not the common practice. Usually the main estimates will contain funding for policies that are yet to receive parliamentary sanction. Supplementary estimates are reserved for funding adjustments identified too late in the preparation process for inclusion in the main estimates and for policies which have been adopted after the budget and estimates have been presented and approved.

While subsequent budget approval procedures are likely to be less rigorous than the original budget approval (and, in terms of their significance, this may be inappropriate) such proposals will often receive some examination by legislative committees. The Australian Senate's estimates committees, for example, allocate a generous proportion (50 percent) of their time to examining supplementary estimates and additional estimates. These will then be embodied in appropriation laws supplementing the main appropriations already agreed to by the legislature and, along with those appropriations, form the total budget approvals for the financial year in question. Legislatures generally must be careful to ensure that they pay appropriate attention to supplementary budget proposals.

APPROVAL – THE SETTING

In principle, supplementary budgets and supplementary estimates should be given legislative effect before the end of the fiscal year to which they apply. To approve expenditure incurred in respect of a year that has already expired is to validate or regularise expenditure retrospectively, since such expenditure had not, by definition, been authorised by the legislature at the time it was incurred. Such excess or unappropriated expenditure is treated in this work as falling into the evaluation and audit phase of the budget process (though a number of countries may refer to it as supplementary estimates).

REVERSIONARY BUDGETS

Finally in discussing the setting for budget approval, it is necessary to advert to a consideration of a point already touched on – what is the position if budget approval is withheld, indeed if a budget is defeated? This involves a consideration of the reversionary budget position.

There are a number of possible outcomes in these circumstances depending upon the terms of the constitution or public finance legislation that is in force in the state concerned.

In an extreme case, failure to pass a budget would mean that when the legal authority provided by the previously approved budget expires any further public expenditure becomes illegal and should cease. But this is a most unlikely outcome. Ameliorating this extreme position there is first the case of expenditure which is authorised on an ongoing basis, whether permanently or for several years beyond the next budget. Failure to pass a particular year's budget would not affect the legality of this spending. It would continue on the same basis as before. Such expenditure can represent a high proportion of total expenditure.

Secondly, the legislature may have granted an interim approval or approvals in anticipation of final budget approval. If so, the government will be able to operate on the basis of these interim approvals even though they may need to be used for longer than had been intended when they were granted. In the worst case, interim approvals may be the only expenditure authority granted in the entire financial year. However, whether interim approvals continue in force if a budget is defeated is a difficult legal question. A former Australian chief justice considered that in his country in these circumstances they might not.[12]

Nevertheless, it is quite likely that the constitution or specific legislation will make provision for a fall-back (reversionary) position if a budget is defeated or has not been passed by a certain date. A particularly favourable rule from an executive's point of view would be for its proposed budget to take effect on a provisional basis. Such a position has been criticised above.[13] It is more likely that the budget approved for the previous year will be deemed by the reversionary rule to continue in effect in these circumstances. This fallback solution retains the status quo in terms of expenditure authority and allows normal government activity to proceed while debate and negotiation continues on the new budget proposals.

The precise reversionary rules can be important in strengthening or weakening the respective positions of the legislature and the executive in any dispute over the contents of a budget (Wehner 2006a). It has been pointed out that if the reversionary outcome differs considerably from the executive's preferred budget, there is greater potential for the legislature to extract concessions from the executive in return for budgetary approval. If, for example, the failure to pass a budget meant that there would be no authority to spend at all, the executive would be highly likely to prefer a compromise to the possibility of government shutdown. In the United States partial government shutdowns have occurred and have proved an incentive for the executive to compromise in budget disputes with Congress. (Though a legislature pushing a budget dispute too far could find its brinkmanship held against it by the electorate too.) Conversely, if the executive's budget proposals take effect or largely take effect even though not yet approved, this can lessen the incentive for it to compromise with the legislature (ibid.).

12. Garfield Barwick, 1995, *A Radical Tory*, The Federation Press, Sydney, pp. 296–7.
13. See p. 50.

4
Approval of the budget – the legislative process

RESOURCES AVAILABLE TO LEGISLATURES IN CONSIDERING BUDGET PROPOSALS

At many points in this discussion the increasing complexity of the budget process and the growth of the information about it have been remarked upon. Members do not necessarily possess any economic or accounting expertise of their own, though no doubt some training in these disciplines could be offered to them. Indeed, in order that members can play an effective role in budget approval and in the further monitoring roles that devolve on them, it would seem essential that they be given at least a rudimentary briefing on the process and introduced to the part they play in it.

Nevertheless, whatever the individual attributes of a member, budget approval and oversight are only two of a multitude of tasks that a member is expected to carry out today. If these budget tasks are to be performed at all adequately, members will require some support. This may be stating the obvious and to a large extent it is. But before discussing the forms which this assistance may take there are three preliminary points which should be made.

Firstly, legislatures will differ in the extent to which they can use and therefore need extensive budget support. Legislatures with a strong role in the budget approval process and which can make a considerable contribution to its composition (Sweden and Germany are examples, and the United States is an even more obvious one) will need sophisticated budget offices of their own or access to the government's resources. Such legislatures can profitably use such resources; indeed, these are essential if the budget role that constitutional or political circumstances enable these legislatures to play is to be fulfilled. Without support they would be unable to do so.

The situation is different with legislatures that cannot, constitutionally or politically, play such a strong role. These are not necessarily 'weak' legislatures. Budget examination and approval may be a politically rigorous and challenging process. But the budget itself is not liable to major alteration or even to any alteration at all as a result of the process. The need for budget resources in such legislatures is much less pronounced and it is less likely that such resources can be productively employed. This is not to say that budget resources are not required at all. They may well be – but not to rewrite or devise a budget. Rather a more modest resource with a greater political orientation may be desirable to help members to use the process of budget appraisal to hold the government properly to account.

Secondly, it is the case that even legislatures that have little influence over the contents of a budget (at the preparation and approval phases) may play a much more significant role in the later evaluation and audit phase of the budget process. At this phase high-level support is required for the Public Accounts Committee or equivalent committees that supervise the carrying out of this role. This is usually provided by the Auditor-General as an officer of the legislature. This form of support will be discussed when that phase of the budget process is addressed.

Finally, although official support is necessary to make budget examination effective where, politically, this is possible, the initiative and involvement of members is still essential to its success. There is a danger that building up an official resource is seen as substituting for member involvement either because of a lack of inclination or of time on the part of members. Indeed, the growth of budget staff and the increasing technicality of the process may discourage the participation of members. This must be avoided. Expertise and resources are an aid to making members effective in their approval and scrutiny roles, but they cannot replace member-involvement itself. Care must be taken in creating a budget resource that this does not displace the role of legislators. If it did it would lack political and moral authority.

Budget offices

The pre-eminent example of a budget office established to assist the legislature is the United States' Congressional Budget Office (CBO) which was established by legislation in 1974. The CBO issues three major reports each year: an economic and budget outlook report, looking at prospects for the next ten years; an analysis of the executive's budget which is available within one month of the budget's presentation; and a report on various options for the budget. The CBO also reports on the costs of other legislative proposals and on longer-term budget-related issues (for example, it has reported on the budgetary implications of an aging population).

The CBO is seen as putting Congress on a more equal footing with the Administration when it comes to exercising budget power. It is regarded as enhancing the credibility of the budget process by revealing and challenging assumptions that would otherwise go unchallenged. In this way it helps to increase transparency and accountability. It also helps to simplify complex budget information for members of Congress. In sum, the CBO may be an essential resource if the separation of powers concept of government practised in the United States is to operate effectively. But while other polities have separation of powers elements to them, Commonwealth legislatures generally do not adhere to this doctrine to anything like the same extent as in the United States. By way of contrast, their systems tend to be parliamentary or mixed presidential-parliamentary.

An important element of the CBO model is that, although it is established as an arm of the legislature, it is independent of direction from either House of Congress as to how it actually goes about its work. Its mandate is prescribed by its constituent legislation and, subject to compliance with this legislation, it determines for itself what functions to perform and how to discharge them.

Uganda has established a Parliamentary Budget Office (PBO) on this model. The PBO was set up as a non-partisan body by a budget law in 2001. It has its own mandate in terms of the legislation and, under the control of its director, it carries out those functions independently of outside direction, even that of the legislature. It is administratively answerable to the Parliamentary Service Commission, but is not answerable to the commission as to how it does its work or for what work is done. Its principal task is to assist Parliamentarians to interpret and understand the budget. It provides information to all committees and can deploy its staff to any committee which requires its assistance. It reports on budget proposals and economic and fiscal forecasts and on all bills with financial implications. It also reports on the implementation of budget measures. While it works with committees, its services are available on request by individual Members of Parliament.

Although an independent office free of outside control, the PBO has successfully identified with legislators. It is taken seriously and used extensively by members and its reports are seen by members as their own (that is, the legislature's) reports. Its views and those of the Ministry of Finance can and have differed. Its interpretation of economic data (even without challenging the accuracy of the data itself) has been different from that of the government. Generally, the PBO does not interact with the media, preferring to relate directly to committees and members, but the director can express an objective opinion to the media on budget analysis if necessary.

Uganda's establishment of a PBO is a most significant step. It was done at a time of single-party government but has endured into the multi-party era. Other African legislatures have been reported as considering establishing budget offices, though so far Uganda is alone in the field. But a different model has been established in the United Kingdom and has been under consideration in Canada.

In Canada the establishment of a Financial Analysis Service has been mooted. In this case the model of an office independent of the legislature has been specifically rejected. The suggestion is that the

APPROVAL – THE LEGISLATIVE PROCESS

service be established within the parliamentary service, not outside it. While recognising the appropriateness of the office of the Auditor-General's status as an autonomous agency not subject to direction as to how it uses its resources, it was felt that the Financial Analysis Service should be organised similarly to the way that legal services are provided to the House of Commons, with decisions on the distribution of its resources made by a committee of the house, rather than independently. This proposal is still under consideration.

The United Kingdom has also followed a more informal path to enhancing the resources available to committees on financial matters. Within the Clerk's Department a scrutiny unit of about 20 staff was established in 2002 to provide specialist legal, economic and statistical analysis for committees. The unit provides staff for joint committees of the House of Lords and the House of Commons and is enlisted to give support to select committees that can benefit from its assistance, particularly in regard to government expenditure, performance reporting and pre-legislative scrutiny. It has also initiated its own across-the-board studies (such as of the adequacy of departmental annual reports) and is developing a special reporting relationship with the Liaison Committee. In regard to the budget process, it routinely briefs committees on the estimates, resource accounts, performance reports and departmental annual reports. Although an internal section within the Clerk's Department, the scrutiny unit has attracted wider attention and has been the subject of recommendations from an outside body that its role should be expanded (Brazier and Ram 2006).

Apart from these more specialised offices that have been established or have been proposed to assist members with financial scrutiny, committees and members have the support of regular parliamentary staff and their library resources. There is also the potential for utilising staff of the audit offices of their respective countries.

Normally audit staff work closely with Public Accounts Committees and this relationship is discussed below. But it is likely that audit staff have skills that could be utilised by other committees in appropriate cases. The House of Commons' Clerk's Department's Scrutiny Unit has a standing arrangement with the National Audit

Office for the secondment to it of an audit staff member, so in this way audit staff are assisting committees other than the Public Accounts Committee in the House of Commons. In New Zealand audit staff regularly assist sector select committees with their estimates and financial oversight functions. In Madagascar any Parliamentarian can approach the supreme audit office (Court de Compte) and ask for an analysis of budget information.

Finally, support for a legislature may come from outside the legislature altogether. This is especially important when adequate in-house research capacity is not available. NGOs may be particularly useful in providing this support by appraising budget information and providing a public input into the legislature's consideration of the budget. (The steps that the legislature can take to encourage this are discussed below.) The Institute for Democracy in South Africa, for example, put in place a Budget Information Service in 1995 to help the fledgling Parliament which had few resources of its own at that time and was working within a tradition of a minimal parliamentary role in the policy-making process. The service produced regular submissions to both national and provincial legislative committees on draft budgets and public finance legislation (Regional Seminar for Parliaments of South-West Africa 2003).

CONSIDERATION OF BUDGET PROPOSALS

Once a government's budget proposals have been outlined to the legislature they, and the supporting budget information, are available for public comment and analysis. It can be expected that, initially at least, this will lead to public interest that is given expression through media outlets. This public contribution to budget consideration is part of the background against which legislative consideration of budget proposals proceeds.

As has been noted above, the precise issues presented to a legislature for decision vary from country to country. But budget approval is, basically, a legislative process, albeit legislation of a very specialised nature. The legislature in approving the budget, in general and in specifics, is being asked to give the imprimatur of legality to the proposals that it contains. Each legislature will have different organisational forms in which it carries out this legislative function, but there is a degree of commonality that can be seen in the processes followed.

Most legislatures will hold a general debate on the floor of the House on the budget presented to it. This may commence immediately or after a short delay intended to allow members to familiarise themselves with the budget's contents. In Malawi, for example, there is a gap of two or three days before the debate gets under way. Many legislatures will have rules giving priority speaking rights to the opposition leader or spokesperson so that the opposition can set out a response to the budget that helps to give shape to the debate. There is, however, a view that the general budget debate is a formality that does not lead to any change in the budget. Its utility is therefore sometimes questioned.

It is undoubtedly true that the outcome of the debate is predictable but it may be looking at parliamentary debate in too narrow terms to write it off for this reason.

The need for legislative endorsement of a budget following a general debate is critically important. If it was not required at all, for example, a government could do whatever it wished. The need to obtain it and to devote parliamentary time to obtaining it makes the point that government is not arbitrary in a parliamentary democracy. Authority for this purpose flows from the legislature to the executive and, regardless of how politically predictable this may be, it needs to be constantly reasserted. Indeed, it needs to be constantly reasserted *because* it is politically predictable.

Furthermore, to criticise the budget because it does not lead to changes is to misunderstand the nature of much parliamentary debate in a party system. No longer (if it ever was) is parliamentary debate primarily directed to changing the minds and opinions of one's fellow legislators (except perhaps on 'conscience' issues when legislators exercise a free vote). Primarily it is designed to state one's own or one's party's position or to expose weaknesses in and force explanations of one's opponents' positions. But a further objective of legislative authorisation of a budget has been seen as a means of establishing benchmarks in relation to which audit takes place. Authorisation by the legislature can be viewed as a 'gateway' to scrutiny (McEldowney and Lee 2005). A budget debate (indeed, the legislature's involvement in budget approval) viewed with these limited objectives may still be judged to perform them poorly. But its utility should be judged on its true aims, not according to unrealistic expectations which it cannot achieve.

Endorsement of the budget in general is admittedly largely symbolic, but it is nevertheless an important symbol.

In a practical sense, how a legislature orders itself for a detailed consideration of budget proposals is likely to be more significant. This will generally resolve itself into a consideration of how effective is the committee system employed by the legislature to carry out this function. The House of Commons formerly resolved itself into a committee to consider budget proposals (the Committee of Ways and Means) and legislatures still from time to time employ this concept of a committee of the whole House with more relaxed procedural rules to consider financial and general legislative business. But the advantages to a legislature of this form of organisation are limited. A more effective form of organisation is found by legislatures appointing smaller committees of members to examine witnesses, consider detailed reports and then report their conclusions on the matters before them to the whole legislature (and, through the legislature, to the public). Only by employing smaller committees can legislatures achieve the in-depth examinations that are essential to their effectiveness. This method of proceedings is now employed almost universally by legislatures, though the comprehensiveness or otherwise of the committee system differs from legislature to legislature.

Committee organisation

A distinction can be drawn between defining committees by the function they perform and defining them by the subject that falls within their remit. The former have a 'horizontal' brief that covers everything to do with that function regardless of the subject matter with which it is concerned. Public Accounts Committees are functional committees of this nature. They examine the public accounts and deal with reports from Auditors-General regardless of the field of government (defence, health, trade, and so on) from which the issue emanates. On the other hand, subject-defined committees have a 'vertical' focus. They deal with matters falling within the particular area of government assigned to them – defence matters, health matters, trade matters, and so on. The nomenclature used to describe subject committees differs between legislatures (sector committees, departmental committees, portfolio committees), and their actual terms of reference, even though subject-based, may give rise to slightly different jurisdictions for ostensibly similar committees. (Thus a 'departmental' health committee may be confined to inquiring into the health ministry and other public agencies dealing with health, while a 'sector' health committee may have 'health' as a subject available to it to inquire into regardless of whether there is a ministry or agency connection.) Nevertheless, in broad terms these two types are alternative forms of committee structure that could be employed to consider the budget's details.

In general, there has been a tendency in budget examination to move away from the functional type of committee towards the use of the sector type of committee. In the United Kingdom, estimates examinations were formerly carried out by an Estimates Committee which was responsible across the board for estimates scrutiny. Now these are carried out by the relevant departmental or portfolio committee – the Treasury Committee for the Treasury's expenditure, the Defence Committee for the Ministry of Defence's, and so on. The Australian Senate has a hybrid arrangement – a number of specialist estimates committees, each with a particular sectoral responsibility.

This move towards sector examination of expenditure proposals is part of a general movement to integrate the review of public sector operations and minimise the distinction between financial and non-financial information concerning performance. Financial operations are seen as merely part of the context in which departments and agencies operate rather than as a separate realm. Whether they are operating effectively and efficiently, whether the policies that they are implementing are justified and contribute to the public weal, is judged in part against what they cost to put into effect. Much less distinction is therefore drawn between authorising expenditure and assessing performance. Indeed, with output- and outcome-based appropriations, performance assessment becomes part of the appropriation process. This is all reflected in a move away from specialist estimates committees to sector-specific committees.

Within this broad approach to committee organisation, legislatures must make choices about how to allocate the task of examining expenditure proposals. One method is simply to disperse responsibility among the sector committees. These can develop an expertise in regard to the area of their own responsibility and can with increasing effectiveness question the implementation of the various programmes within their sectors. On the other hand, this can lead to a lack of detailed attention to the overall fiscal framework, with each committee concentrating on a particular aspect of the budget and no committee having a responsibility for the big picture. Combining the sectoral approach with one that maintains a general fiscal outlook is an attempt to avoid this disadvantage. The overall fiscal framework may be one defined by the government in its budget or (as in Sweden, for example) approved in advance by the legislature. A particular committee such as a budget committee, a finance committee or an appropriation committee is then given the responsibility of overseeing the approval process by committees in its entirety. It may allocate examinations of particular appropriations to sectoral committees, promote standards and consistency, and, importantly, ensures that the various recommendations from those committees are consistent with the overall fiscal framework that has been set. In this way a legislature can carry out its budget approval function in a co-ordinated manner.

The Canadian House of Commons is an example of a legislature that has moved to this model. Even quite recently the Canadian estimates procedure was being criticised for the lack of any overall oversight or examination at aggregate levels. Indeed, not all committees were inclined to carry out their estimates tasks and report on these (Blondel 2001b). Consequently a Government Operations and Estimates Committee was established alongside the sector committees with a mandate to guide and oversee the estimates process. It is hoped that this will combine the best features of the functional and sectoral approaches, ensuring that institutional knowledge of the estimates process is captured systematically and fed back for the use of all committees, while at the same time allowing committees and members with interest and knowledge in the sector concerned to be directly involved in examining expenditure proposals.

Conduct of estimates examinations

A committee structure cannot in itself guarantee an effective outcome to the budget approval process – though a bad structure can prevent one. How the committees go about their work is critical to this.

Some of the factors that impinge on effectiveness at this stage can be identified. Excessive turnover of the members serving on committees has been seen as a problem. This can result from the outcomes of elections causing large infusions of new members. While there are obvious advantages to such infusions (and all institutions need them) there can be disadvantages too in terms of knowledge lost. However, this is the nature of the democratic process. Turnover for this reason must be accepted as a fact of parliamentary life. But where turnover results from members being transferred among committees to suit the convenience of party whips, this is a different matter. While some members will seek such a transfer, others will not and their commitment and experience will consequently be lost. In principle there should be a strong expectation that members assigned to a committee will remain with that committee for the term of the Parliament. There will inevitably be changes that must be made of necessity – for example, if a member is appointed to ministerial office. But parliamentary rules should erect barriers to too easy an ability to shift members around between committees during the course of a Parliament.

Some legislatures may permit any member of the legislature to participate in committee meetings even if not a member of the committee concerned. This is the case for instance in the Australian Senate where a Senator can sit on an estimates committee, but without the right to vote if not a full member of it. This practice can expand the expertise available among committee members for particular examinations.

The chairpersons of all parliamentary committees play central roles in any committee system. Committees which are considering estimates are looking at policy issues. They are quite unlike Public Accounts Committees in this regard (where there is commonly a convention that policy is not questioned);[14] there can be no expectation that policy will not be questioned as part of estimates examinations. Indeed, quite the contrary: estimates hearings will be conducted in a partisan way – even more so perhaps in legislatures with little or no expectation of making budget amendments. In these circumstances the hearings can be seen as very largely an opposition's opportunity to ask challenging questions of ministers and officials. Paradoxically, committees in legislatures where there is a genuine opportunity to make amendments can afford to develop a more non-partisan approach to their work and may have greater prospects of achieving a committee consensus. A judicious chairperson can promote this spirit by the manner in which he or she chairs the committees. With Public Accounts Committees the practice is often (but not universally) for the chairperson to be drawn from the opposition. In the United Kingdom he or she is, in addition, a former Treasury minister. But there cannot be an expectation that a particular party will provide a chairperson for functional or sector committees.

In Malawi (2006) the chairperson of the Budget and Finance Committee is a former Minister of Finance, but this will not always be so. Chairpersonships are sought-after positions, and chairpersons, while not neutral persons, are expected to chair committees in a way that is not patently unfair. For one thing, a chairperson acting in a nakedly partisan manner is likely to provoke trouble in the

---

14. See p. 105.

committee, thus undoing any benefit from cutting corners procedurally. In addition, the chairperson will be expected to encourage members to be attentive at hearings and to participate actively in them, though the extent to which members do participate will differ depending on their seniority and interest.

The support that committees have access to has already been discussed in the context of the legislature's resources generally. The extent to which a dedicated resource such as Uganda's Parliamentary Budget Office can contribute is difficult to exaggerate. Such an office can and should develop a continuous engagement with committees on financial matters. Members with the best will in the world can only do so fitfully. An adequate resource assisting committee members can help to earn the committee the respect of ministers and officials appearing before it. This is important in parliamentary systems since committee members usually exercise the prerogative of questioning witnesses themselves, unlike United States Senators and members of Congress who often allow committee counsel to do so for them. While members taking ownership of the process themselves in this way is to be applauded, it can lead to uneven questioning and interruptions from other members. Contributions from staff to raise the standard of questioning, by briefing committee members and suggesting lines to pursue, are therefore extremely valuable. Committees may also utilise specialised assistance with their budget examinations. For example, in South Africa an NGO researcher has been commissioned to conduct an in-depth gender budget analysis for the legislature (Budlender 2001).

Committees on estimates will almost invariably wish to hear from the responsible ministers and senior officials associated with the proposed expenditures. Experiences can be uneven. It was reported that in South Africa, for example, the Minister of Public Service and Administration failed to attend and did not send a substitute when he had been scheduled to appear before the Finance Committee to consider estimates for the public service (Krafchik and Wehner 2002). While officials are usually not expected to comment on government policy, they may otherwise be asked a wide range of questions. Some analysts see officials as treating the legislature's budget hearings as just another obstacle that has to be surmounted, rather than as a essential and positive exercise (Dobell and Ulrich 2006). Weak parliamentary oversight has helped to contribute to this feeling. Parliamentary performance can in turn weaken the position of officials within government who may be trying to ensure that financial integrity is maintained by promoting effective reporting of expenditure (ibid.). If committees do not evince an interest in such material, less committed officials will be easily persuaded that there is little point in striving for the standards that are being urged on them by their colleagues. Committees must be conscious of the message they send to officials in not taking their examinations of estimates seriously enough.

An important issue for committees to consider is whether to hold public hearings on the estimates that extend beyond the responsible minister.

Committees generally are moving in the direction of involving the public in their deliberations. There is an inevitable and desirable trend in this direction. One reason is that the contribution of civil society can compensate for a lack of budget resource on the part of the legislature (though the legislature will still need a resource to analyse that contribution). Advising the public what is going on before a committee, advertising for submissions and facilitating input of this nature can ensure that a wider range of views on the expenditure proposals is exposed than would otherwise be the case and thus new perspectives can be developed. Especially is this so if relevant experts are approached to contribute their views. One subject that has been identified as benefiting particularly from this input has been gender budgeting initiatives. These have emerged in several countries as a result of partnerships between legislators interested in gender issues and organisations providing relevant research and analysis.

Such contributions could be made at closed hearings but increasingly these are being opened out to allow public and media attendance. Again this is part of a trend to greater openness in the way that legislatures go about conducting their business. Hearings held in public help to inform and provoke debate on the issues under discussion and are seen as a direct counterpart to debates held in the legislative chamber in full public view.

It has to be said that caveats have been entered about the opening up of committee meetings entirely to the public. There is a danger that committee hearings held in public will be more politicised than if they were held in private. Members, it is said, will be more inclined to score points off each other and less inclined to concede the strength of points made that contradict their parties' positions (Regional Seminar for Parliaments of South-West Africa 2003). Paradoxically, it has been claimed that greater media attention will result in a poorer working environment for the committee and less cooperation among members (Dobell and Ulrich 2006; Burnell 2001). This is indeed likely to be the case, though its effect will depend in any particular case on the degree of attention focused on the matter before the committee and how controversial it is. As committee proceedings get more attention, there will be a price to pay and that is likely to be the importation of some behavioural practices more associated with the floor of the House itself.

The other danger that has been identified is a likelihood that as committee proceedings become more transparent, decision-making will shift to other forums, such as caucus, informal working groups or just into the corridor (Regional Seminar for Parliaments of South-West Africa 2003). The first point to make about this concern is that what is being talked of is the holding of hearings – the phase in which evidence is gathered – in public. Committees then have to deliberate on that evidence with the aid of advisers and reach decisions that are embodied in a committee report. Some committees in the United Kingdom (public bill committees) do deliberate in public, but these committees are performing a different function from estimates committees. House of Commons' public bill committees are a means of *debating* an issue, not of *deliberating* on it in an endeavour to reach an agreed committee position. Such a committee is the House in miniature and is really a substitute for a committee of the whole House. Functional or sector committees considering estimates on the other hand are not forums for debate, they are inquisitorial bodies which hear evidence and receive other reports and then form committee conclusions on the basis of that material. If such bodies deliberated in public it is hard to see how the members could work together as committee members to achieve this. It is more likely that in such a case the real decisions would indeed be taken elsewhere and then transmitted to the committee for formal endorsement (this is always a potential danger in any case). So while there are obvious advantages to hearing evidence on estimates in public, deliberating on that evidence with a view to producing a committee report must, if the process is to operate successfully, continue to be done in private.

It is of the essence of the estimates examination that it results in a report from the committee acquainting the legislature, and, through the legislature, the public at large, with its conclusions. Where committees have not been obliged to produce reports on estimates hearings this has introduced a laxity into proceedings that has conduced to a negative view of the entire process. In these circumstances members have shown little interest themselves in carrying out such reviews (Dobell and Ulrich 2006). A requirement for committees to report relatively soon after the estimates are presented is essential. This means that estimates hearings will necessarily be relatively brief and that a full range of other views may not be able to be sought as part of that process. This should qualify the conclusions that committees feel able to draw after estimates hearings. There may inevitably be a certain tentativeness to them. Despatch is inevitable in estimates examinations since the budget approval process cannot be stretched out to too long a time or it may have detrimental effects on the public finance system. If committees feel that matters revealed in estimates hearings need further investigation, this should be reserved for a policy inquiry later.

How committees agree on their reports and whether they permit minority views to be expressed in them are matters for legislative practice generally rather than part of the budget process. One peculiarity of the budget approval process in Uganda is that chairpersons of the various sector committees submit their reports in the first instance to the chairperson of the Budget Committee. Only after the latter approves them are they submitted to the legislature by the several committees. Legislatures can thus experiment with different practices that suit their own conditions.

AMENDMENT OF THE BUDGET

The extent to which the budget is amended by the legislature during the approval phase has been the subject of considerable discussion by parliamentary observers.

In many ways amendment of the budget is the obverse of the degree to which budget approval is considered to be a matter of confidence. In those systems where consideration of the budget is treated wholly or largely as involving the confidence of the legislature in the government, there is correspondingly little or no amendment of the budget. Conversely, in those systems that take a more relaxed view of what involves a matter of confidence, amendment of the budget is more common. In such systems a background factor if the budget is not passed by a certain date is the reversionary position – that is, the extent to which previous financial authorities lapse or continue and thus provide an incentive (or the converse) for a government to compromise on its budget proposals in order to have them approved. However, in all parliamentary systems amendments to a budget form only a minor part of the approved budget. The government's proposals are not only the starting point, they are largely the end point of the process too.

The United States is taken as the paradigm case of a legislature that can extensively amend the executive's budget. In that country the budget has been called 'more a work of fiction than fiscal policy and merely the opening gambit of a long legislative tussle'.[15] Indeed in the United States the legislature does not have only an amending capacity. It can reject a budget and, given its congressional budget resources, construct and impose its own. But the United States is not governed by a parliamentary system and has no concept of 'confidence' or 'responsible' government in a constitutional sense. (The

---

15. 'Fiscal frustrations', *The Economist*, 10 February 2007.

heavy weapon of impeachment may be seen as a partial substitute for this.) Its practices, while of interest as points of comparison, are of limited direct significance to parliamentary systems. Thus envy of the budget influence exercised by congressional committees has been dismissed as unrealistic in such countries as Canada which operate within a framework of responsible government that concentrates not just power but also responsibility in the government of the day (Malloy 2006).

It is true that there is a danger that legislative committees or individual legislators wielding too much power could dilute or obscure accountability for the budget. A concentration of responsibility for the budget solely on the government means that accountability for it is clear. The congressional system has been criticised for fragmenting policy-making and responsibility (Knight and Wiltshire 1977). It may be, however, that some relaxation of power is still compatible with the advantages derived from identifiable budgetary responsibility.

An OECD survey in 1998 found that 97 percent of legislatures surveyed approved the budget without making major changes to it (Sterck and Bouckaert 2006). Westminster Parliaments, by both formal restrictions on amendment and by political practice, experience even fewer amendments than European legislatures where amendment is more common (Schick 2001).

While the lack of ability to amend a budget is today strongly tied up with the idea of confidence, the restrictive rules operated by many legislatures do not originate with that concept. Historically, budget approval was a control process which the Parliament exercised over a government that wished to raise taxes to enable it to put its policies into effect (usually to fight a war). Parliament's role was seen as being to agree or to disagree with the budget proposal, not to substitute one of its own. In these circumstances the formal rules that evolved assumed that taxation and spending proposals would only come from a profligate executive (the Crown or government), that would be restrained by a parsimonious legislature (the Parliament) inclined to protect the citizen from heavy burdens of taxation. Thus the rules began formally to require that taxation and expenditure proposals originate only with the Crown (or its ministers) and to confine Parliamentarians to voting against them or proposing only amendments that would reduce them. What had originated as political practices became rules.

Many of these rules still survive in Commonwealth legislatures. They do express an important principle associated with responsible government. If a government assumes office it exercises executive power and is entitled to do so as long as it remains in office. If a legislature is dissatisfied with the policy being followed by the executive, it has the constitutional power (in a parliamentary system) of dismissing it, but not of taking over executive power itself and imposing its own policy. Executives govern through legislatures; legislatures do not themselves govern.

While this principle is still sound, a case can be made out for some scope for legislative initiative in the budget approval process that does not undermine responsible government. The budget process today is essentially one of policy endorsement. The alternatives that are offered to a government's budget are alternative policies that a party in opposition would like to implement if it achieves power. Given this, most legislators who wish to propose amendments do not want to be confined to suggesting *reductions* in expenditure. The proposing of an amendment in such terms tends to have symbolic significance only, rather than being a real expression of what the proposer wishes to achieve. To this extent restrictive rules obscure political actions. They deserve reconsideration in this light.

Even so, most commentators agree that restrictive rules on what legislators can propose by way of amendment to the budget are not the real reason for the relative lack of amendment of budgets by legislatures. The OECD survey found that constraints on legislative influence are due more to political considerations than to formal restrictions on the power to amend, whether the latter are legal or procedural restrictions. Thus, even if the rules accommodated a broader legislative role, this would not necessarily result in a greater propensity for legislatures to amend the budget. In Canada, under a majoritarian system, little interest was identified in removing formal restrictions or in relaxing political constraints so as to permit legislators a greater role in budget approval (Blöndel 2001a). (The advent of minority government in Canada may have altered this attitude somewhat.)

One obvious constraint on legislatures is a lack of institutional capacity on their part to amend a budget competently. Without the support of a Congressional Budget Office, the legislature's contribution to the budget's details is likely to suffer from lack of informed analysis. The development of legislative resources such as Uganda's Parliamentary Budget Office will assist in developing this capacity. However, merely supplying institutional capacity cannot of itself ensure an independent legislative position on the budget (Schick 2001). Indeed, in a parliamentary system a legislative position that is totally 'independent' of the government is inconceivable.

This does not mean that governments have budgetary carte blanche even in a parliamentary system. A government is always dependent on the political support of the legislature and must ensure that it can deliver it. Thus in Pakistan in 1986 the budget was withdrawn by the government and a new budget substituted when it became clear to the government that it could not guarantee support for its proposals even among its own party members. A change in the political conditions, such as the advent of minority government, can lead to greater overt legislative influence on the budget at the approval stage. Alternatively, this influence can be brought to bear in the course of the budget's preparation and thus obviate the need for amendment of the budget while it is before the legislature. An astute minority government is likely to manage its greater political problems in this way rather than risking embarrassment during the more public approval phase of the budget process.

German parliamentary committees have been singled out as exerting a greater influence during budget approval than other legislatures' committees. This is because the government and the parliamentary majority are not regarded as politically identical in that country and amendment of the budget is not a matter of confidence (Schick 2001). In Westminster Parliaments a greater correspondence between the government and its parliamentary majority is asserted, with the consequence that the scope for the paths followed by the two to diverge is much less.

The fact that legislatures hardly amend the budget should not necessarily be seen as a failing. An effective legislative contribution to the budget process cannot be judged by the degree to which a budget is changed as it passes through the legislature. If a budget were significantly changed that would suggest that its preparation was defective. But the need to go through the process of obtaining legislative approval, with the accompanying accountability obligations that this creates, is justification in itself for a budget approval process. Governments that are confident of their basic legislative support are unlikely to wish to see any weakening of the confidence principle that would enable legislators to vote against budget proposals more readily. Oppositions too are unlikely to wish to accept responsibility for parts of an executive's budget by contributing amendments to it. Even if they were willing to do so the media and the public would have difficulty discerning differing responsibilities if an approved budget was not wholly the government's.

Nevertheless, there is a growing recognition that legislatures can add value to the budget during the approval process and that some potential for amending the budget would in itself stimulate interest and reward participation on the part of legislators and the public in the process. A feeling that the approval process is pre-ordained and futile can undermine willingness to participate. The South African trade union organisation (COSATU) is reported to have refused to participate in budget hearings because the South African Parliament did not have power to change the budget (Krafchik and Wehner 2002). The legislature can itself be a means of bringing the public into the budget process in a way that stimulates public debate to a greater extent than direct public involvement with the government at the preparation stage can. While there is no substitute for contributing to the formation of policy as early as possible (and this suggests contributing at the preparation phase), there is an advantage too in having defined proposals to comment on. At the budget approval phase these defined proposals exist, submissions are not being made in a vacuum. Provided that the public can see some value in participating, the budget approval phase could be opened up to greater participation if limited amendments of the budget were contemplated as an acceptable outcome of it.

To achieve this, formal restrictions on amendments should be reviewed to establish their continued utility. It may be, for instance, that these restrictions should be more concerned with the overall macro effects of the proposed amendment rather than with whether a slight expenditure increase is involved. The committee system in which the budget is considered should be open to public input and some legislative capacity needs to be available to frame suitable amendments. However, above all, political culture will need to change to accommodate a greater prospect of legislative contribution to the budget's details. Whether this can be effected depends upon political factors in each polity.

5
Implementing the budget

A budget that has been approved constitutes a series of policy endorsements and financial authorities. These enable governments to implement those policies and utilise those financial authorities. Implementing a budget is then essentially a government's responsibility. But implementing a budget has much wider consequences and significances than just for a government. The economic and social life of the nation is engaged by the implementation of budget measures and approvals. The way in which these are executed (or, indeed, whether they are executed at all) is thus of considerable interest. This chapter discusses some technical issues involved in budget implementation. The following chapter discusses how legislatures are involved in the financial oversight of budget implementation.

OBLIGATIONS TO IMPLEMENT A BUDGET

Once a budget has been approved the first question that arises is, is there an obligation on the government to implement it?

One might think that this question is wholly moot. If, as has been discussed, it is governments that largely prepare and advocate for budget measures, it would be perverse if they did not implement these once they have been given a legislative go-ahead. If they were not prepared to implement budget measures why would they go to so much trouble to promote them?

In practice, that is largely the answer to the original question. Governments implement budget measures because they considered them so desirable in the first place that they have included them in their budgets and promoted them through the legislature. But it is conceivable that they may have second thoughts after approval is given and may decide that it is not such a good idea after all to proceed with a measure that has been approved by the legislature. In the United States, with its greater opportunities for the legislature to initiate matters for inclusion in the budget, there is also the likelihood that the executive might decide not to utilise expenditures authorised by the legislature because it did not support them in the first place. In that country this is known as 'impoundment'. Impoundment has given rise to disputes between the two branches of government, with Congress maintaining that if it has mandated public expenditure, the President is obliged to execute the law and utilise it.

Essentially, the answer to the question – obligation to implement or not? – is a legal one that will depend on the constitution and other laws of the state concerned and, importantly, on the nature of the measure in question. Here only a few general remarks are offered.

The impoundment disputes in the United States are peculiar to that country's constitutional structure and, in particular, to the strong separation of powers doctrine inherent in it. Impoundment in the United States sense is unlikely to arise in a parliamentary system or in a less strongly separate presidential system. But this does not mean that implementation disputes may not arise.

In general, appropriation authorities are seen as enabling expenditures to be incurred rather than requiring that they must be incurred. This is generally the position in the United States too.[16] If a legislature intends to direct that something be done it does so by using its normal legislative powers, not by merely appropriating funds as part of the budget process. The latter may be an essential concomitant of a legislative direction that something be done; it is

---

16. Michael Foley, 1989, *The Silence of Constitutions*, St Martin's Press, New York, p. 50.

likely to be futile; for instance, to pass a law requiring that something be done without also authorising the necessary expenditure to accomplish it. But the financial authority is a consequence of the legislative direction, it is not the primary motivator of state action itself.

Therefore, one can say that, in principle, budget approval does not in itself oblige a government to implement any measures. But this statement itself also needs to be qualified.

Much of a budget's contents will consist of authorisations to spend money to meet expenditures that citizens have legal entitlements to. Money for social security benefits, development grants, rent rebates, and so on, is included in the budget. It is not for a government to say that it has decided not to spend that money when a person who meets the criteria for payment of a benefit, a grant or a rebate presents himself or herself at a government office and claims it. The government will be under a legal obligation enforceable by a court to pay the benefit, and so on, in those circumstances. Indeed, it is likely to be under an obligation to pay even if the legislature has not authorised the relevant appropriations.

Secondly, even apart from expenditure on entitlements, governments may find themselves obliged to implement budgetary authorisations. If, apart from the budget approval, there is a legislative direction that something be done, a government may be under a legally enforceable obligation to carry out the measure and spend appropriated funds on it even if it has changed its mind as to the measure's advisability. If a government has changed its mind, its proper course is to persuade the legislature to repeal the measure, not to refuse to execute the law. In these circumstances a government may be unable just to refrain from spending money appropriated in the budget; it may be obliged to do so as a consequence of another obligation that the legislature has imposed on it and that a court will enforce.

Thus while one can say that governments are not, in principle, obligated to implement a budget, in practice they will in many instances be obliged to do so because of obligations that exist in law independently of the budget process.

IMPLEMENTATION BY MEMBERS

While a budget that has been approved is essentially a series of financial authorisations given to the government which the government utilises in the process of implementing that budget, members of Parliament may themselves be directly involved in implementing small parts of the budget.

Members are of course likely to be particularly interested in how the concerns of their own constituencies are addressed in a budget. They may therefore advocate for expenditure that is targeted to the localities that they represent. How successful they are will depend on their own standing and the political circumstances of the time. For example, it is said that in France there is a political tradition that allows members with a national profile to obtain certain funds for their constituencies.[17] In this way a constituency can benefit by attracting a national figure to represent it.

Another way in which members (sometimes only members of the governing party) can be involved in budget implementation even more directly is by funds being allocated to them out of the budget for them to spend or allocate on constituency development projects. In this way members of the legislature (even though they may not hold ministerial office) are enlisted into the budget implementation process itself.

While any such system clearly must have safeguards built into it to ensure that funds are used for socially desirable purposes and are ultimately accounted for, the involvement of members can help to counteract too centrist an approach to development and to involve communities at the grassroots in allocation decisions that affect them.

IMPLEMENTATION BY CIVIL SOCIETY

The process of participatory budgeting has been outlined above.[18] Where this process operates the local community is expected to

17. 'Royal wins race to fight for presidency', *Daily Telegraph*, 17 November 2006.
18. See p. 23.

have a role in overseeing the implementation of the projects which it has mandated (Wampler 2000). This may involve local committees being given the authority to approve technical plans and ensure that public works are being carried out in accordance with those plans. Neighbourhood committees can be formed to monitor construction projects on site. Not only does this local participation help to ensure that implementation proceeds according to plan, it can reduce the likelihood of corruption. There have been tensions with governments over this supervisory role with local monitoring committees being weakened by being denied support, thus restricting their ability to track the quality of the work that has been undertaken (ibid.).

REPORTING REQUIREMENTS

An important – indeed, in some ways the most effective – part of monitoring budget implementation is a requirement for the executive to report on how it is implementing the budget. Where this exists such reporting takes the form of reports throughout the year on the progress of implementation, reports at the end of the year both on the implementation of budget measures and on departmental performance, and general economic and fiscal reporting during the course of the year.

An ambitious reporting requirement was enacted in Sri Lanka in 2003, though it has not yet entered fully in force. This requires the government to keep the legislature informed periodically on its progress in implementing budget measures. Parliament can thus keep track of how fully budget plans are being implemented and check on any departure from these. This imposes an unusual requirement on the government to identify positively for the legislature how it is implementing a budget in the course of that implementation.

Most other requirements for governments to report on budget implementation relate to making a review of how budget measures were implemented in the past year. They are thus exclusively retrospective. The Indian finance minister gives an account of action taken on previous budget announcements in delivering the annual budget speech. The Sri Lankan law will require that Parliament be informed whether previous budgetary targets were achieved and budget proposals implemented. Madagascar seems to be unique in requiring not only a quarterly report on budget implementation, but also that at the end of the year the legislature must consider and vote on whether or not the budget has been properly implemented. Budget implementation does not usually require formal parliamentary sign-off.

The annual reports of departments are a prime source for departments to report against the performance targets that they committed themselves to at the beginning of the year. Such reports are therefore coming to include information on service delivery along with the well-established financial statements and audit reports. Guidelines may be promulgated by the government or by the legislature supplementing any statutory requirements as to what annual reports must contain. However, there are doubts about whether members have a high regard for this type of information. One study found little direct evidence of members using performance information in budgets and annual reports in their oversight function, though it may have had a more generalised influence on the opinions that members formed (Sterck and Bouckaert 2006).

The law or practice may require that governments present periodic reports of an economic or fiscal nature linked to the budget approved by the legislature. In Australia a mid-year economic and fiscal outlook (known as MYEFO) is mandated for six months into the financial year. MYEFO is effectively a report card on budget implementation half-way through the budget cycle. Within three months of the end of the year a final budget outcome report must be presented to the legislature describing fiscal outcomes for that year. An unusual reporting requirement is for a statement that reveals the cost in taxes foregone on programmes in which there is a tax concession. The cost of such concessions would otherwise remain hidden. Sri Lanka's 2003 law also requires that a mid-year fiscal position report be prepared reviewing progress on the budget and detailing how the fiscal forecasts on which the budget was based are bearing up. At the end of the year a final budget statement reports on estimated and actual revenues for the year. In the United Kingdom, autumn departmental performance reports set out provisional information on both financial outturns and policy outcomes (McEldowney and Lee 2005).

Election reporting

In an extension of budget reporting some countries require fiscal and economic reports to be presented within a certain time of an election being held. New Zealand requires that the government prepare a pre-election economic and fiscal update between four and six weeks before a general election is held bringing up to date previous economic and fiscal information already reported. The update must be accompanied by a statement of responsibility signed by the Minister of Finance and the Secretary of the Treasury (the senior Treasury official) testifying to the basis on which it is made and that the Treasury has used its best professional judgement in compiling it.

Australia has a similar requirement that the Treasury report on the budget position during an election campaign. In addition, parties can lodge their policies with the Treasury and the Treasury will cost them in fiscal terms and publish its findings.

TRANSFER OF APPROPRIATIONS

A particular issue in the budget implementation phase is the government's ability to use funds that have been appropriated for one purpose for a different purpose.

In some countries it is not uncommon for funds that were originally voted for one purpose to be shifted to another purpose during the course of the year. But any adjustment of this nature raises a question of the legality of such an action. Some flexibility in budget implementation may well be justified to deal with developments in the macroeconomic and fiscal environments as the financial year unfolds. Regardless of legality, frequent transfers of appropriations can be symptomatic of a weakness in the budgetary system evidencing poor economic and fiscal forecasts on which the original budget decisions were taken. For this reason alone close monitoring of governmental expenditure during budget implementation is warranted.

The extent to which governments are permitted to transfer appropriations depends upon the legal provisions applying within the jurisdiction concerned. These may be relatively liberal but there is a tendency to put restrictions on too generous an ability for governments in effect to amend a budget that has been approved by the legislature.

Thus it is likely that there will be rules restricting the range within which an appropriation may be transferred; for example, permitting transfers within a defined category of appropriations (called a 'vote' or 'grant') and prohibiting the transferring of appropriations to other categories. It may be too that only a specified proportion of expenditure (say 5 percent of expenditure within a vote, or a set percentage of the appropriation concerned) may be transferred in this way. It is not unreasonable to limit the ability to transfer appropriations by executive action in this way. If too large a transfer discretion is conferred on the government this would undermine the integrity of the budget approval process since it would always be open to being subsequently set aside by government action. If a government feels that changed conditions warrant a more significant transfer of appropriations than it has legal authority to make of its own volition, it can always present a supplementary budget to the legislature seeking those variations.[19]

It should be axiomatic that all transfers of appropriations must be reported to the legislature. But, in addition, express legislative endorsement or confirmation of appropriation transfers may also be required. If endorsement is required before the transfer can be effected this is in effect a supplementary budget decision rather than a government power to transfer. More commonly, where legislative endorsement of transfers is required, it is given by way

---

19. See p. 57.

of confirmation of transfers that have already occurred and is of the nature of a fait accompli. This is not necessarily an inappropriate weakening of legislative control if there are effective limits on transferred appropriations in the first place. The requirement for confirmation operates to advertise specifically to the legislature the transfer decisions made by the government and to ensure that it is accountable for these. This is the price that governments have to pay for limited flexibility in implementing their budgets.

NEW SPENDING

Linked to transfers of appropriations but logically separate from them is the question of the extent to which governments may initiate spending on matters not contemplated in the budget at all. Thus while most states contemplate transfers between existing appropriations, the question of using part of an appropriation made for one activity on another activity for which no appropriation exists at all is much more problematic. In the former case, the government has received legislative endorsement for engaging in the activity to which the appropriation is to be transferred (although at a lower level of expenditure than it now considers desirable). But in the latter case the government has received no legislative endorsement at all to engage in that activity.

The problematic nature of initiating spending on activities without any legislative authority for them is compounded if no transfer of appropriation is involved at all and the government simply wishes to initiate new spending without savings elsewhere on its overall appropriations. An authority for governments to do this would pose severe fiscal risks and could undermine the budget process altogether. Extensive powers of this nature have been called budget 'amendment authority in reverse' and can lead to executives, during the budget implementation phase, undoing legislative choices made at the time of budget approval (Wehner 2006a).

In principle, governments should not have authority to initiate new spending without legislative authority except in specifically defined circumstances.

One circumstance in which new spending will be warranted is to deal with a major emergency that arises such as an earthquake, a tsunami or another natural disaster. The consequences of such an event will have to be dealt with regardless of budgetary authorisations. In these circumstances what is important is that, after the event, there is a full accounting for expenditures incurred and subsequent legislative endorsement of the steps taken. Indeed, rather than leaving such emergency expenditure to be incurred on an ad hoc basis, budget rules and law can to some extent make provision for the unexpected happening by appropriating a contingency reserve and specifying broadly what it may be used for or by conferring a general authority on the government to incur emergency expenditure, with, in each case, a requirement to account to the legislature for it. A sophisticated set of public finance rules will contemplate that such matters may arise and prospectively provide a means of dealing with them.

6
Evaluation of the budget

Any system of appropriating funds for defined purposes needs to be supported by procedures designed to check how those funds have been used; in particular, to ensure that they have been applied only to the ends approved. The financial system and records supporting the appropriation system should be set up in such a way that these audit processes are facilitated (Knight and Wiltshire 1977). At a basic level, then, budget evaluation involves audit of expenditures incurred as a result of budget approvals to establish that funds have been used lawfully. But budget evaluation involves much more than that.

In practice, budget evaluation is not seen as a discrete process of evaluating the impact and implementation of the preceding budget. This is a very difficult thing to do in any case. There may be no linear relationship that can be drawn between a particular budget and its impact (Balmori 2003). Each budget presents an overlay of measures that add to the impacts resulting from previous budgets and to economic and financial decisions taken by public sector agencies outside the budget process (for example, central bank decisions influencing interest rates). It is hard, if not impossible, to disentangle these influences in assessing the impact of a single budget. (Indeed, for this reason evaluation may not be recognised as part of the budget process at all.) Economic analysis can illuminate these matters and economists and other academic writers may attempt to reach judgments on the economic and social effects of budgets. But legislatures and their committees are most unlikely to try to do so themselves (though they will be interested in the results from others who do so). Such questions can tend to the esoteric for Parliamentarians. As political practitioners they are likely to apply themselves to more limited and definable assessments of how particular policies (whether or not emanating from a budget) have worked. As far as a budget is concerned there are more likely to be contemporaneous *political* assessments of it made by the news media and political commentators. These, however, are likely to be couched in terms of the public's positive or negative reaction to budget measures, with little regard paid to the medium- or long-term effects of them.

These factors mean that the evaluation phase of the budget process is not at all self-contained – indeed, according to some views it does not exist at all. Such budget evaluation as is practised plugs into the general financial oversight processes that are in place and these have an ongoing standing. It is difficult or impossible to disentangle them for a particular budget and not profitable to attempt to do so. Public-private partnerships, for instance, may be entirely divorced from budget authorisations and pose their own problems that are quite separate from evaluation of the annual budget.

Despite having said this, while legislative and media evaluations of budgets as such are therefore somewhat limited in scope, an evaluation phase regarded as part of general financial oversight is seen as a relatively strong aspect of the legislature's budget role. The almost exclusive role of the executive in preparing a budget and the limited opportunities for legislatures to amend or otherwise influence a budget's contents have already been remarked. By way of contrast, parliamentary scrutiny of government expenditure gives legislators greater scope for playing a role in the budget process, certainly as compared to its earlier phases (Brazier and Ram 2006).

AUDITING

Any process involving financial transactions requires a stage of 'attestation' whereby the validity of those transactions is subject to scrutiny. In the case of public expenditure a concomitant public audit process is essential. At the very least this is designed to combat corruption, but its aims go far beyond this. Public audit is a means of promoting improvement in public administration by identifying inefficient and undesirable as well as illegal practices, with the expectation that these inefficiencies and undesirable practices will be addressed and improved or eliminated. Whether there is sufficient follow through in addressing such matters is a subject about which concern has been expressed (this is addressed below).

All departments and agencies should have their own internal systems of audit. These may be wholly internal or include external representation on a body such as an audit committee to bring an expert and impartial perspective to bear on the examination of audit problems. Internal audit is not just a check on those managing the entity concerned, it is a means of assurance to those persons with responsibility that when they certify accounts and financial statements they can have confidence in the validity of the information that they contain. Managers should therefore see effective internal audit arrangements as essential management tools of their own.

While the importance of internal audit may often be overlooked, all countries will acknowledge the necessity of a system of external audit whereby the government's overall accounts and the accounts of individual departments and other public entities are subject to audit by an external party. In most, if not all, countries, states and provinces an official known variously as the Auditor-General, the State Auditor or the Provincial Auditor heads an office that is responsible for discharging this duty. The Auditor-General may be a public servant under the ordinary control of the government or may have a more exalted or protected status than this.

For example, the constitution or another law may make specific provision for the office of Auditor-General and give that officer some security of tenure that is greater than that of a public servant holding office at the pleasure of the government. In some states the Auditor-General may be linked not with the government but with the legislature as an officer of the latter and enjoy a protected status in that way.

In principle, and whatever the precise legal arrangements, the position of Auditor-General is too important to be left purely to the pleasure of the government in office at any one time. In the private sector there have been suggestions that company auditors should not be looked upon wholly as contractors to the board of directors of the company that they are auditing with the potential conflicts of interest that may arise and the weak position that auditors may feel they are in in raising matters antithetical to the board or to those who control the company. There is even less reason to look upon an Auditor-General as a contractor or servant of the government in this sense. Effective public audit is a process that governments should have to endure as the price of holding office, not as a concession offered by them. For the process to operate with integrity the Auditor-General and the Auditor-General's staff should not feel beholden to or subject to instruction from the government other than in ways that are wholly transparent; for example, as set out in the constitution or legislation.

An Auditor-General who is independent enough of the government he or she is auditing is an essential aspect of effective public administration. This includes budget evaluation.

Every Auditor-General will be expected to take a lead in developing appropriate public audit standards. However, there should desirably be external involvement in this process rather than the Auditor-General being solely responsible for setting standards which that officer then implements. Just as the Auditor-General needs standing and freedom from the influence of the government and other agencies that the Auditor-General audits, so there should be a body standing outside the Auditor-General's office that reviews the standards to which the Auditor-General is working. This could be a professional auditing body or an ad hoc committee with auditing and other representation on it that either approves or makes recommendations as to the auditing standards to be followed in the public sector.

Auditing itself has developed enormously in recent decades. No longer is it confined to following a narrow formalistic or legal approach. A much broader, analytic approach is now taken to the task. This has become necessary in any case as countries have changed from the relatively simple forms of cash appropriations to 'resource' or 'output' appropriations which attempt to define what is to be produced as a result of the expenditure authorisation (policy advice, services, and so on) rather than concentrating on the means of producing it (staff, office equipment, and so on). With these changes to the forms of appropriation have come the necessary attempts to define and measure performance standards (speed in processing benefit claims, answering queries, and so on). Audit techniques and practices have had to adapt to measure these new concepts.

Public audit has thus begun to concern itself with how efficiently and effectively particular policies and programmes have been implemented. Without questioning the merits of policy (a matter for governments and legislators), Auditors-General have increasingly been asking: whether a particular policy actually delivered the results it promised, whether it was achieved within budget and on time, what unanticipated inefficiencies in implementing it were encountered, could its objects have been achieved equally well but more efficiently and economically in other ways? These 'value for money' or performance audits have taken public audit far from the narrow preoccupations of previous days. They also call for a much wider range of skills and expertise than just an auditing or accountancy proficiency.

A further important matter to note in respect of public audit is the extent of the Auditor-General's mandate. A responsibility to audit government departments may be taken for granted. But governmental organisation is much more complex than simply taking a departmental form these days. Self-managing (indeed, self-funding) agencies may be created to assume responsibility for the delivery of services formerly in departmental hands. Publicly owned bodies that are expected to operate as commercial enterprises are common, and PPPs, in particular, introduce new dimensions of accountability. Public audit practices have to adapt to these different organisational forms.

FOLLOWING UP AUDITS

Recent developments in public audit and financial scrutiny have been seen as notably successful in a country such as the United Kingdom (McEldowney and Lee 2005). They obviously have much wider significance than just at the culmination of a budget process. They are part of the ongoing financial oversight of government operations. Successive budget processes feed into the system and add new demands to it, they do not stand outside it.

However, there have been concerns expressed about the extent to which the Auditor-General's (and a Public Accounts Committee's) work is followed up. These concerns do not stem so much from that work being ignored and not implemented. Findings in respect of a particular agency are likely to be actioned and faults remedied. Indeed there may be formal processes to ensure this. For example, in Canada departments are legally obliged to set out their plans to address Auditor-General (and Public Accounts Committee) criticisms. These plans are then recorded in the audit report itself (Kelly 2005).

Rather, the concern is about the extent to which general lessons for the public sector are being learnt and absorbed from the extensive audit work that is carried out each year. It is one thing to address particular defects that have been revealed. It is another to use the learning – perhaps from an accumulation of audit reports – and effect systemic change as a result or even (and this is even more difficult to achieve) for these to result in a cultural change within government as to how business is transacted. There is a feeling that these 'deeper' levels of effect are not being reached by Auditors-General. Consequently, mistakes identified in one agency tend to be repeated later or elsewhere in government.

In South Africa this deficiency has led to the suggestion that an agency be charged with designing and implementing curative or preventative measures in response to matters identified by the Auditor-General. It has also been suggested that there be a closer working relationship between the Auditor-General and the Treasury to ensure that issues highlighted in the former's reports can be evaluated and responded to and clear roles assigned to both the executive and legislative branches to achieve this. In this way an Auditor-General's report would not be the end of a process but rather seen as a catalyst for strengthening open, honest and fair government (Krafchik and Wehner 2002).

This is a practical suggestion for addressing a problem relating to the penetration of the lessons learnt from the much more expansive audit processes of today. A 'complementarity' of interest between governments and those concerned with financial oversight in ensuring that public money is spent wisely and prudently has been identified (McEldowney and Lee 2005). But this complementarity of interest can remain potential rather than realised, either through defensiveness (the same authors remark how an 'audit culture' can develop with departments employing auditors and consultants to help pre-empt problems with extensive Auditor-General inquiries) or through an inability to utilise and apply the lessons learned from the audit process. This may be the next major challenge for public audit.

REPORTING

Almost all budget processes of necessity require the government to report on its use of the approvals it has received. These reports may relate to the performance of the government as a whole, to sub-units of the government such as departments, or, increasingly to both. While the reports are addressed or presented to the legislature they are in effect a public accounting by the government to the community on its stewardship of affairs and use of public resources.

Audited financial statements are an essential element of this reporting and have already been noted. But, in addition to financial statements, governments and departments, either by legal requirement or by choice, present a great deal of other information that is essential to a full appreciation of the performance of the public sector in the year or other period under review.

The requirement to prepare and publish a report is likely to be a legal one. The legislation will indicate in general terms what are the matters that the report must address and may even specifically require particular pieces of information to be included or identified (for example, contingent liabilities, contracts over a certain value, and so on). But these requirements are unlikely to be comprehensive and much will be left to the discretion of the reporting entity as to what to include and how to present it. A number of issues thus arise with regard to the contents of reports.

While there may not be a single template for the form that reports take, and there is even some advantage in permitting the various reporting entities to experiment with the design of their reports so that good practices can emerge, it is likely that the government and the legislature will wish to ensure a minimum standard of reporting. Even where legislation is not involved, governments as an internal consistency measure may wish to issue instructions to departments as to how reports are to be prepared and what information is, as a matter of course, to be included in them.

But it is not only governments themselves that have such an interest in the standard of reporting. Legislatures, and especially a sectoral legislative committee with a central government focus, such as a finance or government operations committee, may wish to define in what form they expect reports to be presented to them and what information they wish to receive on a consistent and comparable basis, even without embodying these requirements in legislation. Such a sectoral committee can assume the role of ensuring that the legislature's voice is heard in defining the standards expected of annual reports rather than these decisions simply being made by governments as an internal matter. Ideally, a practice of governments consulting periodically with the relevant legislative committee about reporting standards should be developed. Where particular matters are by law required to be included in a report the failure to address those matters becomes a breach of law and potentially justiciable in a court. But this is a heavy and unsuitable means of enforcing standards. Reporting, whether as part of the budget process or otherwise, is inherently part of a process of *political* accountability.

It is thus primarily for the legislature to assert its prerogatives and ensure that reporting meets acceptable standards.

The failure to present a report at all or within the time that is prescribed for its presentation is also a breach of law amenable to judicial control. But again the aim should be to have effective systems both within government and within the legislature that ensure that such requirements are complied with in the first place, rather than relying on legal action ex post facto. Thus in South Africa the National Treasury has suggested that the legislature become involved in a process of tracking that departments or agencies are presenting their reports to the legislature on time. This involves the parliamentary authorities maintaining a database of all entities that present reports and producing a list each week of those reports that are outstanding (National Treasury, South Africa 2005). As far as conformance with any legal or other prescribed standards is concerned this is a matter that legislative committees examining the reports would be expected to address as a matter of course.

Most reports that are produced will address the government's or a department's performance relative to the targets (if any) that were set for it in its performance plan for the year. South Africa specifically requires each department's accounting officer to prepare an annual financial statement on the implementation of the budget along with a report on the implementation of the department's annual performance plan. These reports must consider the department's performance in terms of implementing its share of the national budget (Mwale 2005).

South Africa too is developing the concept of an 'end-of-term' report in which at the end of the government's five-year term of office each department produces a performance review. The reviews aim to give an overall evaluation of the extent to which departments succeeded in implementing their five-year strategic plans and achieved the overall strategic goals and objectives set for them at the beginning of the period (ibid.). These reports can then inform the strategic planning process that commences for the new term of office after the general election. This type of planning is particularly apposite to South Africa given the synchronising of that country's electoral and planning cycles.[20] It may not be possible to operate a system quite as formal as this elsewhere. Nonetheless, an attempt to report on how government departments performed over the term of a government, provided that objectivity in the reporting process can be guaranteed and the reports do not become simply self-justificatory, is worth exploring.

This last comment raises a general point about all reporting. Requiring an entity to report on a regular basis and defining contents and standards against which that report must be made are essential to ensuring public accountability. But they are not sufficient by themselves. Firstly, there is the question of what is done with those reports by the government, the legislature and society generally. This is addressed below, particularly as far as the legislature is concerned. But, secondly, one must always bear in mind the inherent limitations in a report rendered by the entity under review. It has been remarked that a report or explanation by the responsible official is likely on its own to be inadequate given the likelihood of self-justification and vindication.[21] Reporting that consists of 'hard' data where the figures given in the report can be verified is one thing. But most reporting is not of that nature. It consists of information largely selected by the reporting entity and which is likely to be presented in a way most favourable to that entity. There is nothing improper or underhand about this. It is a natural human response. But it does mean that anyone wishing to make a full judgement of departmental performance needs to be prepared to look beyond the department's annual report.

Once a report has been submitted it is essential that there be some process within the legislature for it to be considered. If there is no process for legislative follow-up this is an open invitation to reporting entities, not just to produce poor reports, but to relax attempts to maintain and improve good public administration. Lack of attention by legislators earlier in the budget process as a potential

20. See p. 119.
21. E. Leslie Normanton, 1971, 'Public Accountability and Audit: A Reconnaissance' in *The Dilemma of Accountability in Modern Government*, ed. Bruce L. R. Smith and D. C. Hague, Routledge, London and New York, pp. 314–15.

encouragement of lax practices has already been identified.[22] If legislators do not have a process for giving reports some attention, the same problem will arise at the end of the process. The United Kingdom's departmental committees now have systematic scrutiny of departments as one of their core functions and they almost invariably undertake annual inquiries into the relevant departmental reports (McEldowney and Lee 2005). But this does not mean that every legislature must conduct a full review of every departmental report presented to it. Given the number of departments and other reporting entities, there may not be time for this. In any case, as has been seen, to be effective a full review of a department must go beyond the department's annual report, thus further reducing the possibility of finding time for a review of all departments in every year.

What is important, however, is that there be a real potential for review and a guarantee that at least at regular intervals the legislature will give its full attention to every department so that its committees can build up a picture of the expenditure plans, administration and operations of the departments falling within their remit. Departments must produce reports in the expectation that they will be subject to parliamentary review, even though they would not know whether this will in the event be so or not. In this way they will be obliged to maintain reporting standards and this can be expected to affect their conduct and the standard of public administration generally.

It is therefore almost invariably the case that departmental reports should be referred to committees for follow-up action. Follow-up could be the responsibility of a specialist committee, such as a committee on governmental operations, the equivalent at the end of the process of an estimates committee (the Public Accounts Committee's work is of a different nature), but increasingly legislatures are establishing a system of sectoral or portfolio committees which carry out follow-up work.

The allocation of a particular report to a sectoral committee may be fairly obvious (the Ministry of Health's report will go to

22. See p. 74.

a health committee if there is one, for example) but the authority to decide on the allocation of reports has to reside somewhere. In South Africa it has been recommended that the legislature establish a process for overseeing annual reports similar to the estimates process and that sectoral (portfolio) committees consider the reports and report back on them in time for the committee conclusions to be taken into account for the following year's budget allocation process (National Treasury, South Africa 2005). This effectively builds legislative committees that are appraising performance into the preparation phase of the next budget. For this purpose, the Speaker would refer reports to the relevant committee and the legislature's rules would define the processes to be followed by committees and the expected outcomes of the process – that is, an oversight report and recommendations regarding unauthorised expenditure (ibid.). In New Zealand a particular sectoral committee (the Finance and Expenditure Committee) is given the role of referring departmental annual reports to the other committees for examination or of retaining them for examination itself (which can occasionally cause conflict with a committee that had expected to have a report referred to it).

LEGISLATIVE EVALUATION

Traditionally the post hoc review function of evaluating public expenditure has been carried out by a Public Accounts or similarly-named committee. (For example, in Australasia not all jurisdictions have a committee called the Public Accounts Committee. However, there is at least one and sometimes two committees in each legislature that carry out functions broadly representative of a Public Accounts Committee (Jacobs et al. 2007).) A Public Accounts Committee is not limited to examining expenditure resulting from the most recent budget or indeed from a budget measure at all (which is why the Public Accounts Committee is not universally regarded as being part of the budget process). One of the distinguishing features of a Public Accounts Committee is this broad government-wide responsibility (ibid.). More recently Public Accounts Committees have (like Auditors-General) moved away from an exclusive concentration on legality to a broader concern with performance. They have begun to question whether the public has received 'value for money' in the way in which policies have been implemented or whether these could have been implemented at less cost or more effectively, or both.

Despite this latter development, the conventions of non-policy engagement by Public Accounts Committees and their close relationship with Auditors-General have been maintained. Public Accounts Committees do not question the policy behind the measure under inquiry. But this has still left important and contentious issues for them to address – legality, efficiency and effectiveness – even if they have not second-guessed a government decision to adopt the policy in the first place. Rather, Public Accounts Committees have been concerned with how in the event the policy was implemented. This restriction on the scope of a Public Accounts Committee's work is an important factor in its likely success in maintaining an effective parliamentary oversight of a government's financial activity (Stapenhurst et al. 2005).[23] Without it such legislative work may not have been done at all or may have been frustrated by political contention.

Other legislative committees may also carry out a financial oversight role, either under a specific reference from the House or as part of a general authorisation with a brief to keep the performance or activities of departments within a certain sector under review. But these committees are not constrained by any conventions requiring them not to question policy.

Indeed, the reviews by sectoral committees are often a means of *challenging* policy. There is nothing surprising in this. Members generally find policy work more to their taste than the somewhat drier review work associated with pure financial oversight (Sterck and Bouckaert 2006). The former is a means of putting forward proposals that may have their origin in a party's policy and is seen as a clear

23. See Appendix 3 for an analysis of Public Accounts Committee performance.

means of effecting change. The latter can be highly technical and not clearly linked with making a difference (though it may lead to new policy being devised as a reaction to defects it reveals). Apart from the general predilection of politicians towards policy, legislatures would be strange bodies if a large number of their committees followed a practice of not questioning policy. Legislatures are expected to challenge policy; that is the stuff of politics. Following a convention of not questioning policy must be the exception, not the rule, and be reserved for those aspects of parliamentary work where it can clearly add value, such as for Public Accounts Committees. To attempt to extend the convention into the work of other committees would be unrealistic and inappropriate.

The role played by Public Accounts Committees as compared with sectoral (policy) committees must therefore be differentiated, though, as will be seen below, attempts have been made to link their work to achieve a more effective general legislative evaluation of budget implementation. (Indeed, some Public Accounts Committees, or committees carrying out public accounts functions, may have estimates scrutiny functions too. One study found that in five out of ten Australasian jurisdictions, such committees performed ex ante budget approval functions in some form (Jacobs et al. 2007).)

EVALUATING PUBLIC-PRIVATE PARTNERSHIPS

Public-private partnerships (PPPs) have already been discussed in terms of their budgetary implications.[24] A concern at the evaluation phase of the budget process is how legislatures perform their role of holding those implementing them to account.

There are two major issues that have been identified.

One is in dealing with claims to commercial confidentiality. PPPs are particularly prone to raising problems of this nature because they by definition involve the private sector. But if information that is critical to an assessment of the performance of PPPs is withheld,

24. See p. 53.

legislative committees will be unable to make informed judgements on them. Claims to commercial confidentiality for information has been seen as seriously inhibiting accountability and calls have been made to make full disclosure to committees a condition of entering into a PPP (Brazier and Ram 2006).

But the other difficulty that arises goes to the very basis on which an assessment of performance of a PPP would be made.

It is, of course, beyond the scope of this book to establish what this basis should be. Some analysis has been done of the performance of projects subject to PPPs. It has been said that from an economic and financial perspective the benefits of PPPs are still uncertain, though some sectors (roads and bridges) fare better than others (information technology). There are also questions about the practicability or appropriateness of PPPs in areas where there is a high expectation of social obligation (for example, hospitals) (Hodge and Greve 2007). Apart from these questions of economic and financial evaluation and social applicability there are other questions of social equity and service that legislators are concerned with generally when any public service is involved. Legislative evaluation of PPPs needs to find means of engaging meaningfully on these issues. It cannot be said that any policy has yet been devised to meet the problems posed by these questions.

PPPs thus raise different challenges to those where a straightforward review of services provided wholly from within the public sector is involved. This has led to calls for the legislature to examine how it can keep pace with these developments and ensure that its means of scrutiny are effective in dealing with them (Brazier and Ram 2006).

ROLE OF COMMITTEES

As with the detailed work on estimates, it is inevitable that committees will be at the forefront of the legislature's financial oversight role.

While legislatures could employ specialist financial oversight committees (the Australian Senate, for example, uses its estimates committees for part of this task), most assign this work to sector committees with responsibility for particular subject areas. These sector committees will almost inevitably have other responsibilities of a policy nature (such as legislation) and this will limit their ability and inclination to pursue their financial oversight responsibilities (Dobell and Ulrich 2006). Members themselves seem to rank this oversight role relatively lowly, after constituency interests, helping individuals, and legislative policy formulation, for example (Malloy 2006).

Despite these disadvantages it is difficult to exaggerate the importance of the oversight role. In Canada, some legislators are reported as having apportioned at least part of the 'contextual' blame for the scandal that led to the Gomery inquiry into government sponsorship and advertising on inadequate parliamentary oversight (Dobell and Ulrich 2006). Vigorous parliamentary examination of departmental plans, budgets and performance would, they believe, have helped convey to ministers and officials that Parliament was paying attention to financial management. It might also have helped to identify the kinds of programmes that are most susceptible to misuse of public resources and encouraged Parliament to strengthen its oversight in those areas. In fact a variety of factors unrelated to the issue itself (including a change of Prime Minister and an impending election) brought this issue to the fore, rather than parliamentary activity (ibid.). This can be seen as a parliamentary failure.

Although financial oversight can be seen as part of the budget process, there is no particular time limit within which it is carried out. It may even be part of the budget implementation phase if it relates to activities undertaken during the current financial year or is a review of the annual reporting of governments and departments carried out shortly after the end of that year.

Canadian committees have been criticised for not paying attention to their financial oversight role throughout the year and for not linking the planning and performance information in the estimates to their policy studies (whether these are carried out as part of budget monitoring or otherwise), though exceptions have been identified where links have been made (ibid.). The first of these criticisms is an obvious danger for a committee with a number of responsibilities. Legislation and other inquiry work of a policy nature is likely to take priority and financial oversight does not get done until it absolutely needs to get done, at the end of the financial year when financial outturn figures and annual reports become available. The second results from a failure to see a link between the performance information that is now commonly made available and programme concerns that may emerge independently. This echoes the low interest generally that members seem to take in performance information in annual reports.

The first problem is essentially a workload issue – can sector committees adequately cope with the different streams of parliamentary business? There can be no one answer to this. The Australian Senate has until recently divided these responsibilities. Estimates committees scrutinise annual reports thus relieving the sector committees of this responsibility. The sector committees themselves were formerly divided between legislation committees and inquiry committees (with the latter able to perform some financial oversight roles). However, these legislative and inquiry functions of the sector committees have now been amalgamated and the new general purpose committees will have to resolve priorities between these various types of business.

Establishing more explicit links between the planning and performance information that is available and the policy studies carried out by committees should be possible. Partly this can be done by improving the support available to committees, enabling researchers to find out what links there are and bring those to committees' attention. Otherwise, seeing parliamentary operations on a 'whole-of-Parliament' basis has been suggested. Thus South Africa's National Treasury has suggested a division of responsibility and collaboration between the Public Accounts Committee and sector committees that has promise (National Treasury, South Africa 2005). Under its proposal, sector committees would concentrate on service delivery, with a heavy focus on performance, and their conclusions would serve as inputs for the work of the Public Accounts Committee. Conversely, the Public Accounts Committee would communicate to committees its views on specific issues that it considers they should be aware of (indeed, the Auditor-General could do so too). Finally, a sector committee could work in association with other sector committees. Their work would then feed into the work of the Public Accounts Committee (ibid.). A well designed committee structure is an essential factor in enabling legislatures to exercise effective budget scrutiny in the implementation and evaluation phases (Wehner 2006a).

A whole-of-Parliament approach such as that suggested in South Africa and by commentators will not be easy to establish. A legislature is not a monolithic body. Committees are likely to be jealous of the relative degree of autonomy given to them. Individual members have differing objectives and motivations in carrying out their functions. These are not necessarily directed to co-operating with other parliamentary actors. Nevertheless, a greater awareness of what other arms of the legislature have done and of the information available should help to improve overall parliamentary performance.

PROCESS OF COMMITTEES

The South African National Treasury in guidelines that it issued in 2005 has suggested that Parliament develop a process for overseeing annual reports similar to that for the budget approval phase. Committees would consider the reports and report back on them in time for this to be taken into account for the following year's budget allocation process. This would tie the implementation and evaluation phases of one budget into next year's budget cycle (National Treasury, South Africa 2005).

To implement this, it recommended that the clerk of the Parliament maintain a database tracking the fulfilment by departments of their reporting obligations. The Speaker would refer annual reports to the relevant committee. Committees would be charged with producing an oversight report. They would be expected to seek the views of ministers, particularly where there is evidence of poor performance or poor audit outcomes and the minister is required to take appropriate steps. However, it is not the legislature's role to resolve management problems, that is for the executive to do. The legislature would focus on accountability for performance and check that the executive has acted appropriately to deal with identified problems. The committees would also hold public hearings before producing their reports (ibid.). Many Parliaments do follow a practice of having sector or other types of committee conduct reviews of annual reports.

Most (but not all) Public Accounts Committees are chaired by an opposition member as a matter of convention. This is less likely with sector committees. In Trinidad and Tobago three independent Senators are chairs of committees, and in the Australian Senate, with its former division between legislative and inquiry committees, government Senators chaired the former type of committee and opposition Senators the latter. But, just as conventions on not examining policy are inappropriate for such committees, there can be no necessary expectation that chairpersonships will be shared. This will depend upon political circumstances in the country concerned or whether any wider parliamentary conventions about sharing chairpersonships are developed.

Specialist assistance from persons with a particular knowledge of the areas being scrutinised can clearly be valuable to committees in performing their financial oversight role. In the United States the division between budget and audit assistance is expressed in the two congressional offices that have been established, the Congressional Budget Office and the Government Accounting Office. The former's few equivalents have been discussed above. The latter equates to the assistance most legislatures receive from the Auditor-General. This assistance has generally been channelled through the Public Accounts Committee. Indeed, a close working relationship with the Auditor-General has been identified as a critical success factor for Public Accounts Committees (Stapenhurst et al. 2005). But the assistance of the Auditor-General could be valuable to other committees making inquiries into performances as part of financial oversight. The extent to which the Auditor-General's office's resources are available to other committees is therefore of importance where the evaluation of budget measures is carried out by sector committees. To date this appears to have been relatively limited perhaps due to the strong link with Public Accounts Committees and a feeling that it is inappropriate to expand these further than this. This assumption (if assumption it is) deserves to be questioned. It may be that Auditors-General can expand their contact to sector committees without endangering their reputations for impartiality.

The extent of examinations carried out by committees is largely a matter for them and will depend upon competing priorities. This is a perennial problem for busy legislators. Often standard questionnaires are developed for departments to respond to, to supplement information provided in the annual report. Indeed, these questionnaires may lead to changes in reporting standards themselves, by information they have requested in the past being incorporated into reports in the first place. Questionnaires thus need to be kept under annual review to ensure that they are not duplicating the information already presented in the reports presented to the legislature.

An interesting suggestion made in South Africa is for portfolio committees of the national Parliament that are examining annual departmental reports to bring into consideration the annual reports of provincial departments in the same sector. In this way the full impact of national policy implementation in that sector can be considered. It has also been suggested that the committees convene meetings with equivalent committees in the provincial legislatures to start the process of review (National Treasury, South Africa 2005). It is not apparent that this suggestion has yet been implemented. South Africa has a particularly integrated federal-provincial planning and reporting system so would be expected to be in the vanguard of any such developments. Other countries do not have such closely integrated national–sub-national budget or planning processes and their constitutional arrangements may not be conducive to the national legislature taking the lead suggested in South Africa.

UNAPPROPRIATED EXPENDITURE

The approvals given by the legislature up to the end of the financial year or other period to which those approvals relate constitute the authorities for public funds to be committed to those purposes. The use of public funds for purposes not encompassed by those approvals or the expenditure of moneys in excess of the amounts approved is, subject to a government's legal power to transfer appropriated amounts to other purposes, unlawful. Excess or unauthorised expenditure may occur deliberately or inadvertently. It may be identified by the government itself or be revealed in the normal process of auditing government activities. Significant illegalities are likely to be the subject of a report by the Auditor-General and come to the attention of the Public Accounts Committee.

Unlawful expenditure of any kind is a matter of concern. The integrity of the budget process and, even more, the rule of law depends upon there being clear legislative authority for the expenditure of public money. However, there is particular concern where unapproved expenditure is a large component of public spending, even if steps are subsequently taken to validate this. A large disjunction between budgeted expenditure and actual expenditure suggests a systemic deficiency in governance arrangements. In one example from 1997, authorised budget expenditure was 31 percent underexpended. At the same time 25 percent of actual expenditure had never been authorised as part of the budget process (Burnell 2001). In these circumstances the budget process was seen as something of an academic exercise, since the difference between what the legislature was approving and what was actually happening was so extreme. In such a case there is clearly a major problem with the effectiveness of a country's budgetary process.

Most unauthorised expenditure will not evidence a systemic problem of this scale, but it may be evidence of a laxity of control or of a culture of non-compliance with what is, after all, the law. (It may also be a result of more technical matters. In the United Kingdom, since the introduction of resource accounting, a considerable proportion of the excess expenditures that have arisen have been caused by changes in the valuation of assets – appropriations now being required for intangible movements of that nature (Lee 2004).)

Any unlawful expenditure that is revealed will require the authorities to consider taking action to recover the expenditure. This may involve initiating a prosecution or surcharging the individuals concerned. Where there is evidence of corruption or extreme carelessness, such action will be justified. If this occurs on a large scale, specific inquiry either by a legislative committee or a commission of inquiry with judicial powers may be appropriate. However, unappropriated expenditure does not only, or even mainly, arise in these ways. It arises from inefficiencies, inadequate monitoring, mistakes and poor systems. The Auditor-General will be concerned to reveal these and suggest ways of eliminating or reducing them. But this still leaves the question of the unlawful expenditure to be accounted for.

Most legislatures are therefore presented with legislation to validate expenditure or write off losses from the previous financial year. In a sense this forms a signing off of the public accounts relating to that year by the legislature. The expenditure submitted to the legislature for validation in this way will usually have been the subject of a report by the Auditor-General. In addition, the Public Accounts Committee and any relevant sectoral committee may have examined the expenditure. In South Africa it has been specifically recommended that a portfolio committee in reporting on a department should make recommendations as to how any unauthorised expenditure is to be dealt with (National Treasury, South Africa 2005).

The process of validating unlawful expenditure should never be merely an academic exercise. Apart from the culture of non-compliance with appropriation rules that this might promote or appear to be endorsing, approval of unappropriated expenditure should be seen to be part of a process of continuous improvement. As a condition of validating expenditure legislatures should look for assurances that steps have been taken within government to reduce the likelihood of the same thing happening again. Often a Public Accounts Committee's or the Auditor-General's report will be a catalyst for such improvement. The extent to which the public sector learns from this process and internalises good practice in consequence has already been discussed. But a rigorous legislative process for considering unauthorised expenditure and treating it with the seriousness that it deserves, is an essential part of a process of improving public sector performance.

A particular concern arises if unappropriated expenditure is not submitted to the legislature for validation until a considerable time after the expiry of the year to which it relates. This delay will often arise because of the time that is taken to produce final public accounts for the year in question and to audit them. The solution will therefore often lie in improving the efficiency with which these operations are carried out. (Though in the United Kingdom the appropriation procedure was itself identified as a barrier to the closing of accounts, and steps were taken to address this by changes to the way in which Parliament authorises supplementary appropriations (Lee 2004).)

In principle, reaching a final account of the previous year's public finance outcomes should be achieved at the latest during the course of the next financial year. It should not be allowed to drag on. However, instances have been identified of excess expenditure being submitted for legislative validation up to six years after it was incurred. In these circumstances the legislature is faced with a fait accompli in approving it and there is a suspicion that officials know this and that that factor has contributed to the delay in submitting the expenditure to the legislature.

An efficient appropriation process, good accounting and auditing facilities to ensure that financial information is available in a timely fashion after the year ends, and strong legislative requirements for final outturns of the public accounts to be produced to the legislature must be insisted upon. These should be conditions of budgetary approval.

7
The federal dimension and second chambers

The simple paradigmatic case for studying the budget process is of a budget being presented to the House of a unicameral legislature of a unitary state. In such a case there are no federal/state relations to be considered and no role for a second chamber to be brought into the mix.

But the majority of countries in the Commonwealth do have one or both of these elements. They are either federations with the almost inevitable consequence of there being a second chamber populated on the basis of state or provincial representation or, even if not a federation, have a second chamber (or upper House) with some role or potential role in the budget process. A consideration of these factors and how they impinge on the budget process is therefore necessary.

This study is principally concerned with national budgets. The main point of interest in this chapter is therefore how federal systems or second chambers influence the national budget process. However, it is worth considering first how a federal system, in particular, influences sub-national budgeting, for there is more evidence of this 'top-down' effect than of a 'bottom-up' effect of sub-national executives and legislatures influencing the national budget. Second chamber influence introduces a different dimension.

Arrangements for sharing out central government revenues to states and provinces in Australia and Canada have already been noted.[25] In Australia this formerly took place on an annual basis as a result of meetings between the federal Prime Minister and finance minister and state premiers. While these meetings still take place, the division of revenue is now made on a more structured basis as a result of a formula applied by a commission to the raising of revenue from goods and services tax. Provinces in Canada are relatively autonomous in their revenue-raising powers but a similar formulaic approach (embodied in law) is followed to share out items of expenditure between the federal and provincial levels of government in areas of shared constitutional responsibility.

Other federal countries have similar standing arrangements to share out revenue or have established forums for the taking of such decisions. Thus in Malaysia the constitution provides for a National Finance Council to co-ordinate important matters of federal and state finance. The council is chaired by the Prime Minister and consists of the Minister of Finance and the chief ministers of the various states. In practice, problems of federal-state finances are often resolved at an official level and embodied in formal understandings between the Minister of Finance and the chief minister of the state concerned. In India, states collect taxes and duties (other than income tax) in their own right and receive funding from the union government under strict guidelines based on performance and programmes. Much of this support is automatic, otherwise it is subject to negotiation between the union government and the state governments. State budgets are presented to the Central Planning Commission chaired by the Prime Minister and composed of eminent and expert persons who bring their own judgements to bear on budget proposals, subject to general guidelines set by the union government. The commission cannot veto or change a state budget, though it can suggest changes. It has no history of acting in a partisan manner or under government direction. Each state legislature considers the state budget following the review carried out by the Central Planning Commission.

While in all federal systems there are likely to be such formal and informal arrangements to ensure some co-ordination between

25. See p. 9.

federal and state budgeting there are always likely to be difficulties in achieving consistency between the different levels. Thus it is quite conceivable that contradictory macro-economic approaches may be being followed simultaneously by the federal government and a state government, especially ones of different political persuasions. How far these budgetary policies diverge and for how long this obtains will depend upon the legal framework within which the federation operates (a federal government may have the legal power to refuse to allocate funds to the state so as to force it to change its policies or a state may have no independent sources of revenue) and political circumstances (a politically weak federal government may not feel strong enough to challenge a determined state government). A further political dimension to federal-state budget relations that has been identified, is to diffuse or share political responsibility (which is inherent in a federal system in any case). Thus it has been speculated that proposed economic reforms in Mexico conferring increased sales tax powers on the states are intended, in part, to effect desirable though unpopular fiscal changes while passing the political cost on to the states.[26] How far this is true is, of course, a matter of opinion.

However, where federal-state budget linkages do exist they generally do so between federal and state executives, without direct legislative links (South Africa is an exception to this).

To a large extent, diversity is inherent in a federal system anyway and so some differences in budgetary approach are inevitable, even desirable. But the strongest attempt in constitutional terms to align the provincial budgetary processes with the national budget process appears to be that in South Africa under its post-apartheid Constitution. That Constitution sets out principles of what is referred to as 'co-operative government' involving all levels – national, provincial and local. In accordance with these principles an attempt has therefore been made to align the planning and implementation of budgets at the three levels (Mwale 2005).

An important, indeed critical, factor in this alignment is the synchronisation of the electoral cycle in South Africa. National and

---

26. 'Having his cake and eating it', *The Economist*, 23 June 2007.

provincial elections are held simultaneously in South Africa every five years. This contrasts with most other federations where the electoral cycle for the national Parliament is likely to be quite different to those for state legislatures and where the electoral cycle of each state legislature is likely to be quite different from that of every other state legislature. Indeed, there is no guarantee that the parliamentary terms will be the same at each level or from state to state.

South Africa's simultaneous elections do not mean that the same election result obtains nationally and in each province. This simply does not occur, though the differences in party representation in each legislature are probably much less than in systems where national and state elections are uncoordinated. But simultaneous elections do mean that in budgetary planning terms the nation and its provinces can start from the same point. This is done by linking the strategic planning process to the electoral cycle. After each election every national government department is charged with developing a five-year strategic and performance plan setting out goals for the department as a whole and strategic objectives for each of its main delivery areas (these are linked with the medium-term economic framework). These plans become major factors in making annual budget decisions. In developing the plans, ministers and officials must consult with their provincial counterparts. The latter in turn must ensure that their strategic planning is consistent with national goals and is informed by and linked to development plans produced by the local government units in their provinces. Provinces are thus seen as being constrained in their choice of policies but retain freedom to develop innovative ways of managing the implementation of these (Mwale 2005). The national Parliament may also integrate provinces into its consideration of budget measures. Thus the National Treasury has recommended that sectoral committees of the national Parliament should consider the annual reports of provincial departments in assessing the full impact of national policy implementation. Indeed, it suggested that meetings be convened with committees of the provincial legislatures for this purpose (National Treasury, South Africa 2005). In addition, a budget council comprising national and provincial finance ministers also includes the chairpersons of parliamentary finance committees throughout South Africa in an endeavour to align national and provincial budget policies.

South Africa has thus attempted to integrate its budgetary process, at least at a strategic level, through a national process that is informed by provincial and local views including those of legislators.

This system of co-ordinated national planning also provides an example of a 'bottom-up' contribution to national planning through the requirement for consultation between national and provincial departments. However, the effectiveness of contributions of this nature to national strategies can be hard to assess since it is merely a further part of the background against which national policy decisions, including budget decisions, are taken. (This has been discussed in Chapter 2 on budget preparation.)

In most countries generally there does seem to be little direct contribution to national budgeting from state and provincial executives or legislatures, though, no doubt, the latter can make their views on such matters known directly to national governments or through the media if they choose to do so. On the other hand, states and provinces may play a formal part in the national budget process insofar as some second chambers may explicitly or implicitly assume a role of representing state interests as a 'State's House'.

The extent to which second chambers do play such a role is disputed. The growth of political parties at a national level has in many ways diluted the specific political significance of geographical representation from different states. Most electoral systems of course retain geographical representation. Members do represent their own constituency's interests and these can be discernibly different from those of other parts of the country. But these differences of interest, where they exist, are often overlaid by a national policy or view transmitted through nationally organised political parties. The scope for local divergence from a party line may be quite limited. This is true too where legislators are indirectly elected by state legislatures. Such differences as exist are also often confined to a locality or small group of localities rather than reflecting a peculiarly state or provincial view. It can be difficult to identify differences of interest between one state and its neighbouring states (other than emotional identifications expressed through sport, for example). Where there are significant ethnic, economic (for example, natural resources) or cultural differences and these coincide with state boundaries, real distinctions can exist at the sub-national level. But here the underlying distinctions are not the different states as such but those deeper identities. Thus while there may be different sub-national interests there is no inevitability that a second chamber will represent these better or more distinctly than a single popularly elected chamber. In these circumstances even a second chamber elected on an avowedly state basis may cease to represent specifically state interests (or may do so in a weakened sense). It can therefore come to be merely a differently constituted part of the legislature, albeit one with a political view that, because it is differently constituted, is slightly or even fundamentally at variance with the more straightforwardly or popularly elected chamber.

There is thus little evidence that the roles that second chambers play in the budget process (greater or smaller depending upon the country concerned) represent a peculiarly state perspective; popularly elected chambers are equally able to represent different geographical or local budget perspectives. Perhaps the second chamber that best reflects a State's House perspective on the budget is South Africa's National Council of Provinces which does consider provincial finances. The National Council of Provinces has a partial rotating membership comprising members of provincial assemblies, thus giving it a close identification with the provincial assemblies themselves. But this is unusual – most second chambers are not populated from state or provincial assemblies (India's Rajya Sabha is another). The most dramatic example of a second chamber's influence on the budget occurred in the Australian Senate which, in 1975, by not passing the budget, was able to engineer the dismissal of the government. But its actions had nothing to do with different regional or state opinions. It was composed of members of national political parties just like the lower House, the House of Representatives, but in different party proportions, so that the governing party, in a majority in the House of Representatives, was in a minority in the Senate. The power that the Senate exercised was exercised on a national, not a states, basis.

If second chambers in the main tend not to represent any distinctive sub-national views, that does not mean that they do not have a part to play in the budget process, as the example of the Australian Senate demonstrates. But the extent to which they have a role to play will often be constrained by the constitution or by law. In an extreme case, such as that of the United Kingdom's upper House, the House of Lords, its approval of the budget may not be necessary at all. By law, if the House of Lords has not approved a 'money bill' (which covers, but is not limited to, budget bills) within one month, the bill can be presented for assent into law.[27] (However, this does not mean that that house does not contribute to consideration of the budget. The fullest analysis of the United Kingdom's annual tax measure is 'paradoxically' undertaken by a committee of the House of Lords, though it does not seek to amend such a bill (McEldowny and Lee 2005)). Other constraints may not be as drastic as this but they may, for example, remove any formal power of amendment from the second chamber, otherwise constrain its power to consider a budget, or at least require that budget proposals be presented to the lower House first.

As a general rule, it may be surmised that a second chamber's formal and effective role in the budget process depends largely on how that chamber is populated. An unelected chamber such as the House of Lords has no democratic mandate to second-guess the House of Commons on something as important as a budget (though it took a major constitutional crisis in 1909–10 finally to establish this). In Pakistan an indirectly elected Senate has only recently been conceded a role even in discussing budget proposals and making its own recommendations on them. In Canada an appointive Senate, in practice, chooses not to challenge the budgetary supremacy of the elective House of Commons. On the other hand, a second chamber which is fully elected may (if its legal power to do so is left intact)

---

27. *Erskine May's Parliamentary Practice*, 23rd edition, p. 929.

feels no compunction about challenging the other chamber on budget matters. There is a political dynamic at work here. Recent discussion on reforming the composition of the House of Lords is likely to bring in its wake a re-examination of the law and conventions that govern its relationship with the House of Commons on budget matters if the former becomes wholly or partly elective. A joint committee report in 2006 concluded that if the House of Lords acquired an electoral mandate, its role as a revising chamber and its relationship with the House of Commons would inevitably be called into question.[28] A composition that is wholly or partly democratic is likely to give a chamber greater confidence in asserting a role in the budget process.

Subject to specific exceptions such as that of the presently constituted House of Lords, where a budget requires legal endorsement by the second chamber (as most will) it must pass through the appropriate stages in that chamber after being approved by the lower House. While the generally less popularly elected nature of second chambers will mean that the budget proposals are given a more cursory consideration by the latter, this need not be the case. Once again, the Australian Senate stands out in this regard. Parliamentary budget scrutiny in that country is indeed primarily undertaken by Senate committees (Sterck and Bouckaert 2006). Only Senate committees, for example, carry out estimates (and supplementary estimates) examinations for which purpose the estimates are remitted to one of eight committees. In India, the second chamber, the Rajya Sabha, participates with the Lok Sabha in joint committee examinations of estimates.

The second chamber's contribution to the budget process, then, while generally less important than that of the popularly elected chamber, can vary enormously depending upon its political standing and legal powers.

---

28. *Joint Committee on Conventions – First Report* (2006), para. 61.

8
Reflections

This book has been concerned with 'the budget process'. In this chapter a few reflections will be offered on that process arising out of the previous discussion and from what may be identified as the expectations associated with the budget process.

A first point that becomes particularly apparent when one considers how a budget is evaluated concerns whether it is indeed a discrete process. We have become used to budgets being presented to and approved by legislatures on an annual basis and this suggests a process with a beginning some months before budget day and a termination some time after the fiscal year ends when all relevant reports have been prepared and have been considered by Parliament. But in practice the process is not as tidy or so contained as this. Its beginning is certainly not precise; it is more like trying to find the source of a river. In the event, there is no one commencement point to preparing a budget just as there is no one source to a river. The continuous flow of public business does not switch over at one certain point in time to the next budget. Decisions and considerations accumulate as influences and inputs into budget preparation in a largely undifferentiated way. The phases of the budget process thus come to resemble peaks in a continuum of public activity rather than separate projects within government. At the conclusion of the process too there is little that can be identified as a formal termination of it. Financial oversight as practised by legislatures through Public Accounts Committees and sector committees is not exclusively concerned with the immediately preceding budget. Rather, that budget provides the latest overlay of measures that form the subject matter of financial oversight by legislatures. For this reason it can legitimately be argued that there is in many legislatures little or no formal evaluation of each *particular* budget, even where there is strong financial oversight of the accumulated stock of budget measures that have been actioned over time.

The annuality of the budget process must be qualified too. In the United Kingdom an annual appropriation statute as a cornerstone of the House of Commons' power in financial matters has been traced to 1869 (Lee 2004), though some annuality was a budget feature even before this date. It is as unprofitable to explore why an annual period was chosen for actioning budgets as it is for much other activity that is actioned on an annual basis. There is a 'natural' appropriateness that attaches itself to annuality but in respect of budgets, while the principle of annuality still obtains, longer-term perspectives have been introduced. The attempts to link budgets to medium-term strategies and economic forecasts are examples of this. These developments are relatively recent. But everything in the public realm of an economic and financial nature is not necessarily renewed in the annual budget and this has been the case historically. Permanently appropriated expenditures go back to at least the salaries of judges in the early eighteenth century, and other appropriations may be made on a multi-year basis to give certain programmes and activities greater funding assurance than that deriving from an annual vote. Taxation and other sources of revenue are likely to have an ongoing continuity in most countries, only being attended to by an annual budget when the government wishes to propose changes to them. It has been said that budget formulation for any one year starts from what already exists (Knight and Wiltshire 1977). Each year is not 'year zero' in revenue and appropriation terms. Indeed, because much expenditure is effectively committed through previous obligations that the state has entered into, the influence that governments can wield in respect of public finance through a single budget may be extremely constrained.

The budget process is a legal process. It is the means by which the bulk of public spending is given legislative endorsement.

However, unlike most legal processes the route of accountability for it and of enforcement of it is not to the courts but to the legislature itself and its agencies (such as the Auditor-General). Courts are very rarely involved in construing appropriation legislation as opposed to other legislation passed by Parliaments. In a sense, the purely legal aspect of the budget process is de-emphasised in deference to its political significance. This is no bad thing. It reflects the working involvement that legislatures have in the approval and evaluation of budget measures. The legal requirements that may be associated with budget matters (such as when it must be presented, what information must be presented with it, what form departmental reports must take) therefore tend to be enforced by political action within the legislature itself. The budget process is still relatively free of judicial control, even in an era of otherwise increasing judicial review of the public sector's activities.

The budget process can be seen too as a policy process whereby governments present policy choices for formal legislative endorsement. This is certainly an important part of the budget process and the part that the legislature plays in financial oversight should, it has been said, evolve from a formal expenditure review to one that focuses on an analysis of policy and administration, the former being subordinate to the latter (McEldowney and Lee 2005). The changes to the form that appropriations take away from a concern with cash or inputs to a focus on the outputs or objectives of engaging in public expenditure and the consequent development of means of measuring performance, support this suggested evolution. The budget process provides a means for governments to present contestable policies for public debate.

If the budget process is free of legal technicality and litigation, it is of central importance as an aspect of *governance*. Indeed, this can be seen as being at its core. An effective budget process is a test of the effectiveness of a country's governance processes. This, of course, begs the question of what is an effective budget process and different analysts of budgetary practices will have their own views on this. One major issue over which discussion of the effectiveness of legislative scrutiny of the budget has arisen is the extent to which a legislature in practice can amend the executive's budget. A legislature which does not have a practical capacity for doing this cannot according to some views be an effective legislature and this will consequently mean that the budget process is in an important respect flawed, because budget approval becomes a formality (this issue was discussed in Chapter 4).

It is the thesis of this book that this does not necessarily follow.

There are, of course, major differences between presidential or congressional and parliamentary systems as to legislative capacity in budget approval. Where the separation of executive and legislative power is a strong feature of a country's constitutional arrangements, the legislature will be more independent of executive influence and may have a pronounced budget-amending capacity. The United States is the prime example of such a system. But this does not mean that budget approval, much less the entire budget process, has little or no legislative point in parliamentary systems. That point, it is suggested, is as an attempt to ensure that there is good governance.

The budget process, though an important (perhaps the most important) government activity, is only one activity of government. It is unrealistic to expect that the legislature will be able to process a budget with a freedom from executive influence where that influence operates as an essential part of the polity's general constitutional or political background. It is political and constitutional norms of behaviour (rather than law) that will determine how a legislature exercises influence over the budget. If these norms involve the executive as a participating and largely controlling element of the legislature (a typical Westminster system), then executive influences will inevitably be brought to bear on how the legislature considers the budget, just as they are brought to bear on how the legislature carries out its other functions, such as passing general legislation. Governments with a legislative majority will find it easier to pass legislation than those without such a majority. They will find it easier to pass their budgets too.

In a fused or largely fused executive/legislative system the executive depends upon the support of the legislature, but the legislature is not thereby free of executive influence. Indeed this dependence necessitates executives seeking to influence legislatures. The executive is itself a (large) part of the legislature. It is not a body that is in some way alien to the legislature. Constitutionally, it is an integral part of it. Its members have been elected and represent the public just as much as do non-ministerial legislators. In a presidential or congressional system where these factors do not obtain, legislative influence on a budget, in contradistinction to the executive's influence on it, can be correspondingly different.

In most circumstances it should be no surprise that the views of a focused, usually dominant, group within the legislature, the government, will generally prevail. Not only should it be no surprise, this is likely to accord with public expectations (governments are expected to govern), and to instil some coherency and consistency into policy-making (a unified group of relatively like-minded individuals making policy, rather than shifting allegiances within a more diverse assembly). Such a group then assumes responsibility for the policies that are adopted.

This does not mean that executive control of how the legislature processes a budget needs to be total. Even in many parliamentary systems this is not the case. Budgets can be amended 'around the edges'. A challenge for governments and legislatures is perhaps to find ways of conceding the ability of Parliamentarians to add value to a budget while it is passing through the legislature, without promoting an undue defensiveness on the part of the government. In some countries (for example, Malawi) this legislative ability may already be part of the political culture. In others (for example, Canada) it has been identified as desirable and steps are being taken to develop it. But its absence does not indicate a failure of liberal democracy. The author of a comparative analysis of legislative influence and control over budgets, while finding substantial variations in these, concluded that the presence of a strong influence or control was not everywhere a fundamental element of liberal democratic governance. It could be important for some countries while in others the legislature's budget control was maintained as an agreeable constitutional myth without the latter countries ceasing thereby to be successfully functioning democracies (Wehner 2006a).

But if an actual, independent legislative power to amend a budget is not fundamental, a budget process that exposes the executive's proposals to scrutiny is. It is in this respect that the budget process as a critical, perhaps fundamental, contribution to good governance is made manifest. A requirement that governments regularly present a comprehensive budget programme to the legislature, accompanied by explanatory information and forecasts (preferably in the context of a previously adumbrated economic and fiscal strategy), is, or should be, an essential governance discipline. It is critical that there be an ability for the legislature to examine and criticise those proposals with help from civil society and its own advisers, but not necessarily to substitute its own policies for them. It is critical that it be a requirement for governments to submit to audit and reporting obligations with further possible legislative scrutiny so as to make government operations transparent and require governments to account for them. These factors, it is suggested, are what a good budget process should be concerned with – establishing an infrastructure of good governance.

Some of the components of this infrastructure and how they could be improved or enhanced have been discussed in this book. These improvements or enhancements include:

- legislative committees should hold pre-budget hearings; legislatures as the representatives of civil society should endeavour to channel legislative and public opinion on the budget into the government's consideration of budget preparation;
- the conventions on budget secrecy need to be reassessed and relaxed with a view to establishing their utility and applicability (particularly in the light of freedom of information principles);
- the legislature or its lead finance committee should be fully involved in considering changes to the form in which estimates are presented;

- 'permanent' authorisations of expenditure should be conceded only if there is a compelling justification for this; such authorisations should be kept under review for their continued applicability;
- interim authorisations of expenditure are, in general, an unsatisfactory means of approving expenditure for any lengthy period of time; their use should be closely circumscribed;
- better definitions of public-private partnership models be devised; legislatures be involved in approving financial commitments for these;
- members should be expected to remain with a committee to which they have been assigned for the term of a Parliament; parliamentary rules should prevent them being reassigned too easily in the course of a Parliament;
- formal restrictions on amendments to the budget should be reviewed to ensure their continued utility; they should be more concerned with the overall macro effects of the proposal than with slight expenditure increases;
- parliamentary consideration of the budget should be opened up to public input and some legislative capacity created for amendments to be framed;
- legislatures must insist on the presentation to them of information on financial outturns in a timely fashion after the fiscal year ends;
- legislatures need to establish appropriate means to evaluate the performance of public-private partnerships.

However, it must be conceded that a good infrastructure alone will not ensure honest and wise practices, much less successful outcomes. Many other factors of a cultural, social, economic and international nature enter into the mix. In longer-established democracies, budget procedures may have become somewhat embedded and taken fairly rigid forms. However, even in such democracies this study has identified some openness to change in respect of the amendability of budgets and vast improvements have been made to the information accompanying them. For more recently established democracies, political culture may be more fluid and there may be greater opportunities for legislators to mould the budget process in ways that promote good governance without undermining effective executive government – for example, by conceding legislatures a greater role in the construction of budgets than they enjoy elsewhere. But in all cases proposals for adapting the budget process should be assessed in the light of the constitutional and political practices in place in the state concerned rather than as the application of a general doctrine of how budgets should be processed. The budget process is nothing if it is not pragmatic in its practices.

Appendix 1
Works consulted

Balmori, Helena Hofbauer, 2003, 'Gender and Budgets – Overview Report', BRIDGE (development – gender), Institute of Development Studies, University of Sussex, February

Beaumier, Guy A., 2006, 'The Accountability Act and the Parliamentary Budget Officer', Economics Division, Library of Parliament, Canada, 29 June

Bishop, Hon. Julie, 2006, 'Australia's Commitment to Gender Equality', *The Parliamentarian*, Issue Three

Blöndel, Jón, 2001a, 'Budgeting in Canada', *OECD Journal on Budgeting*, Vol. 1, No. 2

Blöndel, Jón, 2001b, 'Budget Reform in OECD Member Countries: Common Trends', *OECD Journal on Budgeting*, Vol. 2, No. 4

Brazier, Alex, and Ram, Vidya, 2005, 'Inside the Counting House – A Discussion Paper on Parliamentary Scrutiny of Government Finance', Hansard Society

Brazier, Alex, and Ram, Vidya, 2006, 'The Fiscal Maze – Parliament, Government and Public Money', Hansard Society

Budlender, Debbie, 2001, 'Review of Gender-Budget Initiatives', Community Agency for Social Enquiry, http://www.internationalbudget.org/resources/library/GenderBudgetpdf.2001

Burnell, Peter, 2001, 'Financial Indiscipline in Zambia's Third Republic: The Role of Parliamentary Scrutiny', *Journal of Legislative Studies*, Autumn, Vol. 7, No. 3

Cowan, Hon. Justice E. K., 2004, 'Parliament and Economic and Financial Management – Good Governance in Sierra Leone', *The Parliamentarian*, Issue Four

Dobell, Peter, and Ulrich, Martin, 2006, 'Parliament and Financial Accountability' in *Commission of Inquiry into the Sponsorship Program and Advertising Activities – Restoring Accountability – Research Studies: Volume 1*, Canada

Hodge, Graeme A., and Greve, Carsten, 2007, 'Public-Private Partnerships: An International Performance Review', *Public Administration Review*, May/June

[133]

International Monetary Fund, 2001, 'Report on the Observance of Standards and Codes. India – Fiscal Transparency', 23 February

Jacobs, Kerry, Jones, Kate, and Smith, David, 2007, 'Public Accounts Committees in Australasia: The State of Play', *Australian Parliamentary Review*, Autumn, Vol. 22, No. 1

Kelly, Dr Joanne, 2005, 'International Perspectives on the Role of National Legislatures in Public Finance Oversight: Key Issues and Consideration', paper presented at Nha Trang, Vietnam

Knight, Kenneth W., and Wiltshire, Kenneth, 1977, *Formulating Government Budgets – Aspects of Australian and North American Experience*, University of Queensland Press

Krafchik, Warren, and Wehner, Joachim, 2002, 'The Role of Parliament in the Budget Process', Institute for Democracy in South Africa

Lee, Colin, 2004, 'Supply Motions and Bills in the House of Commons: The Impact of Resource Accounting and Budgeting', *The Table*

McEldowney, John, and Lee, Colin, 2005, 'Parliament and Public Money' in *The Future of Parliament: Issues for a New Century*, ed. Philip Giddings, The Study of Parliament Group

McGee, David, 2002, *The Overseers: Public Accounts Committees and Public Spending*, Commonwealth Parliamentary Association and Pluto Press

Maseko, Hon. Lindiwe Michelle, 2006, 'The Role of Parliamentarians in Gender Budgeting', *The Parliamentarian*, Issue Three

Malloy, Jonathan, 2006, 'The Standing Committee on Public Accounts' in *Commission of Inquiry into the Sponsorship Program and Advertising Activities – Restoring Accountability – Research Studies: Volume 1*, Canada

Mwale, Linda, 2005, 'The Process and Oversight of a Financial Budget in South Africa', *Forty-Second General Meeting of the Society of Clerks-at-the-Table in Commonwealth Parliaments*

National Treasury, South Africa, 2005, 'Guideline for Legislative Oversight through Annual Reports', 26 January

Pollitt, Michael, 2005, 'Learning from the UK Private Finance Initiative Experience' in *The Challenge of Public-Private Partnerships: Learning from International Experience*, ed. Graeme Hodge and Carsten Greve

Regional Seminar for Parliaments of South-West Africa, 2003, 'Parliament and the Budgetary Process, Including from a Gender Perspective', 26–28 May

Roberts, Hon. Matthew, 1999, 'A Big-Screen Presentation – Information technology Enhances Saint Lucia's Budget Address', *The Parliamentarian*, October

Rubin, Marilyn Marks, and Bartle, John R., 2005, 'Integrating Gender into Government Budgets: A New Perspective', *Public Administration Review*, May/June

APPENDIX 1

Schick, Allan, 2001, 'Can National Legislatures Regain an Effective Voice in Budget Policy?', *OECD Journal on Budgeting*, Vol. 1, No. 3

Stapenhurst, Rick, Pelizzo, Riccardo, and O'Brien, Mitchell, 2005, 'Scrutinizing Public Expenditures – Assessing the Performance of Public Accounts Committees', World Bank, http://www.econ.worldbank.org/

Sterck, Miekatrien, and Bouckaert, Geert, 2006, 'The Impact of Performance Budgeting on the Role of Parliament: A Four Country Study', 2nd Transatlantic Dialogue, Leuven, 1–3 June

Wampler, Brian, 2000, 'A Guide to Participatory Budgeting', http://www.internationalbudget.org/resources/library/GPB.pdf.2000

Wehner, Joachim, 2006a, 'Assessing the Power of the Purse: An Index of Legislative Budget Institutions', *Political Studies*, Vol. 54

Wehner, Joachim, 2006b, 'Effective Financial Scrutiny' in *The Role of Parliament in Curbing Corruption*, ed. Rick Stapenhurst, Niall Johnston and Riccardo Pelizzo, World Bank

Wehner, Joachim, and Byanyima, Winnie, 2004, *Parliament, the Budget and Gender*, Inter-Parliamentary Union, United Nations Development Programme, World Bank Institute, United Nations Fund for Women

Appendix 2
Participants in the CPA Budget and Financial Oversight Workshop, London, 8–10 November 2006

MEMBERS

Senator Hon Parvatee Anmolsingh – Mahabir, Trinidad and Tobago
Hon. Robert Nason Bondo, Malawi
Senator George Brandis, Australia
Hon. Nizar Dramsy, Madagascar
Hon. Nisar Ali Khan, Pakistan
Hon. William Okecho, Uganda
Shri Suresh Prabhu, India
Hon. Frédéric Rasamoely, Madagascar
Hon. Sagala Ratnayaka, Sri Lanka

COMMONWEALTH PARLIAMENTARY ASSOCIATION

Hon. Denis Marshall, Secretary-General
Mr David McGee, New Zealand
Ms Meenakshi Dhar
Mr Anthony Staddon

WORLD BANK INSTITUTE

Dr Rick Stapenhurst
Ms Lisa von Trapp

COMMONWEALTH SECRETARIAT

Dr Indrajit Coomaraswamy

BUDGET, FINANCE AND ECONOMY COMMITTEES, UGANDA

Hon. William Okecho, Chairperson, Budget Committee
Hon. William Nsubuga, Chairperson, Finance Committee
Hon. Lubega Kaddunabbi, Chairperson, Economy Committee
Hon. Henry Banyenzaki, Deputy Chairperson, Budget Committee
Hon. Betty Olive Kamya

PARLIAMENTARY BUDGET OFFICE, UGANDA

Mr Wanyaka Samuel Huxley, Director
Mr William Lubowa, Senior Data Analyst

Appendix 3
Scrutinising public expenditures: assessing the performance of Public Accounts Committees[1]

Rick Stapenhurst, Riccardo Pelizzo and Mitchell O'Brien

INTRODUCTION

In 2002, David McGee wrote a comprehensive report on two important elements in the system of public financial accountability, namely the office of the Auditor-General and the parliamentary oversight committee commonly referred to as the Public Accounts Committee (PAC).[2] In this report, based on the deliberations of a Study Group organised by the Commonwealth Parliamentary Association (CPA) in 2001,[3] McGee examined current practice across the Commonwealth regarding the roles and functions of Auditors-General and PACs and the interaction between these two institutions.

The purpose of the original Study Group was to assess how PACs were operating and whether they are fulfilling expectations as important guarantors of good governance. In particular the Study Group attempted to draw upon practice in order to develop checklists for Parliaments to consider or in order

1. This appendix updates and expands World Bank Policy Research Working Paper No. 3613 (May 2005) written by Rick Stapenhurst, Vinod Sahgal, William Woodley and Riccardo Pelizzo.
2. David McGee, 2002, *The Overseers: Public Accounts Committees and Public Spending*, Pluto Press, London.
3. The Study Group was supported by the World Bank Institute.

to improve or refine the operation of their own PACs.[4] When undertaking this analytical process the Study Group started from the premise that social, economic and political factors within each country mean that there is no one organisational model that a PAC should take. In addition, the Study Group discussed and sought to define a modern rationale for PACs, necessitated by the greater interdependability of nations today, which pose greater challenges to good and honest government.[5]

In his report, McGee sought to identify possible courses of action to improve governance and accountability outcomes through more effective use of PACs. The three main priorities he identified in order to bring about more effective PACs were:

1. *Capacity-building*
   Improving the ability of Parliaments and their PACs to carry out their functions by providing them with adequate resources, training and access to relevant expertise.
2. *Independence*
   Ensuring PACs and Auditors General were free from political or legal constraints that could inhibit them from carrying out their duties diligently.[6]
3. *Information exchange*
   Facilitating the exchange of information and ideas so that PACs are up to date with important developments, changing standards and best practices as they emerge.

The purpose of this appendix is twofold; to deepen McGee's analysis of PACs and to expand on the analysis contained in the 2005 Policy Research Working Paper (PRWP).[7] In particular, this appendix defines successful PAC performance and identifies those factors which facilitate or hinder successful performance. It draws upon data collected by the World Bank Institute (WBI),[8] using a survey questionnaire sent to over 70 national and state/provincial

---

4. The terms 'Parliament' and 'legislature' are used interchangeably throughout the appendix.
5. Commonwealth Parliamentary Association, 2001, *Report of the Study Group on Public Accounts Committees* held in Toronto, Canada, 28–31 May 2001.
6. This priority was noted to be particularly important for Auditors-General.
7. Rick Stapenhurst, Vinod Sahgal, William Woodley and Riccardo Pelizzo, 2005, *Scrutinizing Public Expenditures: Assessing the Performance of Public Accounts Committees*, World Bank Policy Research Working Paper No. 3613, World Bank, Washington DC.
8. In collaboration with the World Bank's South Asia Financial Management Group.

Parliaments in Commonwealth countries in Africa, Asia, Australasia, Canada, the Caribbean, the Pacific and the United Kingdom in 2002.[9] Fifty-five usable responses have subsequently been received by the WBI, which is a much larger sample than that originally used in the 2005 PRWP.[10] Supplementary interviews (both in person and on the telephone) have been conducted to seek further insight and clarification of the survey results.

In section 1 of this appendix, a summary of the role of Parliaments in financial oversight is provided, along with a general description of public financial accountability. The critical role PACs play in financial oversight is emphasised, noting their origin in the nineteenth century and their widespread use throughout the Commonwealth and elsewhere.

In section 2, the survey instrument is presented and the broad findings of the survey are summarised. The data collected by the WBI since the publication of the 2005 PRWP have further deepened our understanding about how PACs work and, in particular, what – in the views of the Chairs of these committees – constitutes successful performance and what factors or conditions influence such performance.

In section 3, the success factors (and constraints) for PAC effectiveness are considered, using the survey results. In section 4, possible benchmarks for measuring the effectiveness of PACs are identified, and how developing countries may be able to think about strengthening their PACs is discussed. Finally, in section 5, the appendix draws some conclusions and proposes what an ideal PAC might be like.

1: PARLIAMENTS AND PUBLIC FINANCIAL ACCOUNTABILITY

1.1 Role of Parliaments

Parliaments have three primary functions – representative, legislative, and oversight. They perform a representation function in that they represent the will of the people, which is the legitimate source of authority in democratic countries. They perform a legislative function because, in addition to introducing legislation on their own, they have the power to amend, approve or reject government bills. Finally, and most importantly for the purposes of this appendix, Parliaments perform an oversight function, ensuring that govern-

9. For a comprehensive list of Commonwealth countries please refer to the Commonwealth Secretariat website, http://www.thecommonwealth.org/.
10. When the original PRWP was drafted only 33 usable responses had been received. Therefore, this appendix draws upon a sample 166 percent larger than the original PRWP.

ments are held accountable for the policies and programmes they implement. They undertake this oversight function in two ways: they oversee the preparation of a given policy (ex ante oversight) or can oversee the execution and the implementation of a given policy (ex post oversight).

Though most Parliaments have the power to keep the government accountable for its actions and its policies, there is considerable variation in the legislative tools that Parliaments can employ when performing their oversight function. This variation reflects to a large extent differences in the form of government and other constitutional arrangements. These tools include parliamentary committees, parliamentary question time, interrogations, urgent debates, the estimates process, scrutiny of delegated legislation, private members' motions and adjournment debates that allow Parliamentarians to raise issues relating to the use or proposed use of governmental power, to call upon the government to explain actions it has taken and to require it to defend and justify its policies or administrative decisions.[11]

One of the tools that Parliaments can use to further enhance oversight of the financial operations of government is a specialised committee. In the 'Westminster model' of democracy,[12] the specialised committee is known as the Public Accounts Committee, or PAC; it is the 'audit committee' of Parliament, and therefore the core institution of public financial accountability.[13] As Frantzich pointed out more than two decades ago, Parliaments need useful information to perform their representative, legislative and oversight function effectively.[14] It naturally follows that PACs similarly need

11. See Riccardo Pelizzo and Rick Stapenhurst, 2004, *Tools of Legislative Oversight*, Policy Research Working Paper No. 3388, World Bank, Washington DC.
12. The term 'Westminster model of democracy' was developed by political scientist Arend Lijphart. According to Lijphart, 'the term *Westminster model* [is used] interchangeably with *majoritarian mode* to refer to a general model of democracy'. See Arend Lijphart, 1999, *Patterns of Democracy*, New Haven, Yale University Press: 9. This model of democracy is defined by: concentration of executive power in one-party and bare majority Cabinets, Cabinet dominance, two-party system, majoritarian and disproportional systems of elections, interest groups pluralism, unitary and centralised government, concentration of legislative power in a unicameral legislature, constitutional flexibility, absence of judicial review, a central bank controlled by the executive.
13. In some countries such as India and Sri Lanka the Public Undertakings Committee coexists with the PAC to cover the oversight of autonomous public enterprises.
14. Stephen Frantzich, 1979, 'Computerized Information Technology in the US House of Representatives', *Legislative Studies Quarterly*, 4(2): 255–80. See also Robert Miller, Riccardo Pelizzo and Rick Stapenhurst, 2004, *Parliamentary Libraries, Institutes and Offices: The Sources of Parliamentary Information*, World Bank Institute Working Paper No. 33040, World Bank, Washington DC.

useful information to function effectively. The primary source of information for PACs is generally provided by the legislative auditor, or Auditor-General. The auditor reports to the Parliament and the public at large on whether public sector resources are appropriately managed and accounted for by the executive government.

1.2 Concept of public financial accountability

Following implementation of a government's budget, a legislative auditor audits government accounts, financial statements, and operations. In most countries, this audit is followed by consideration of the audit findings – which may include value for money and performance auditing as well as financial or compliance auditing – by the Parliament. If Parliament's role in the budget process is effective, parliamentary recommendations to the executive, based on the deliberations on the audit findings put forward by the auditor, are reflected in future budgets, thus allowing for continuous improvements in public financial accountability.

The exact nature of the relationship and interaction between Parliament and the auditor partly depends on the model of the legislative auditor and the reporting relationship between the auditor, Parliament and the PAC. In most Commonwealth countries, the legislative auditor is the Auditor-General, whose office is a core element of parliamentary oversight; he or she reports directly to Parliament and the PAC. In some instances, the Auditor-General is an Officer of Parliament, which guarantees his or her independence from the executive (as in the case of Australia and the United Kingdom); while in some other instances he or she is independent of both the executive and the Parliament (as in the case of India).

The structure and function of the PAC date back to the reforms initiated by William Gladstone, when he was British Chancellor of the Exchequer in the mid-nineteenth century. The first PAC was established in 1861 by a resolution of the British House of Commons. Replicated in virtually all Commonwealth and many non-Commonwealth countries, PACs are seen as the apex for financial scrutiny and have been promoted as a crucial mechanism to facilitate transparency in government financial operations (see Figure 1).

Across the Commonwealth, however, there is considerable variation in PACs' terms of reference and modus operandi. In some instances, for example, the terms of reference are narrowly defined; in these cases PACs concentrate exclusively on financial probity. In other instances, the terms of reference are more widely defined; here, the committee does not simply focus on financial probity but also on the efficiency and effectiveness of programmes in achieving the objectives for which they were established. In fact, as will be detailed more comprehensively later in this appendix, the

FIDUCIARY OBLIGATION
Parliament

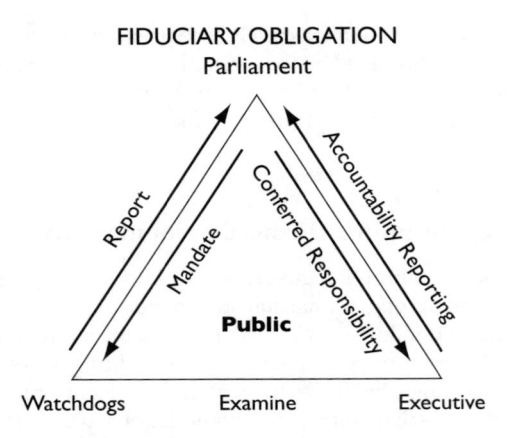

Figure 1: Parliament's accountability function

'scope of work' is one of the principal factors affecting PAC performance. There is considerable variation, too, regarding the relationship between the Auditor-General and the PAC, the status of the PAC within Parliament, how the PAC conducts its business, reporting arrangements between the PAC and Parliament and on requirements for government follow-up on PAC recommendations. Moreover, these and related issues are examined in detail in McGee's original 2002 report. An important feature in virtually all jurisdictions is that PACs do not question the desirability of a particular policy – that is the mandate of parliamentary departmental committees. Rather, PACs examine the efficiency and effectiveness in the implementation of policy.

Although McGee outlined *how* PACs work, in an effort to identify good practices across the Commonwealth, he did not consider, in any detail, the *reasons* behind the good practice – what might be called the critical success factors or why some PACs are considered more successful than others. Conversely, McGee did not identify constraints hindering the performance of PACs in less successful cases. This appendix explores such issues in greater depth.

2: SURVEY RESULTS – OVERVIEW

In the survey undertaken by WBI, PAC Chairs were asked to self-assess the impact of their committee's work, with some of their responses summarised in Table 1. It would appear that PACs are most successful acting as a catalyst for improvement in government implementation of policy decisions and for improvement in the availability of government information to Parliament. In 69.4 percent of cases, PAC Chairs state that the government responds favourably to committee recommendations, while in 56.3 percent of cases, governments implement such recommendations. Typical, perhaps, is India, where, over the period 1980–99, the government accepted 60.7 percent of recommendations made by the PAC.[15] Similarly, in 55.3 percent of cases, PAC recommendations have improved the availability of information to Parliament. However, the survey findings show that PACs are less frequently the catalyst for the government to change legislation or major policy objectives or to prosecute officials who break the norms of probity or present misleading financial information to the public. One notable exception is Uganda. Since the mid-1990s, the Ugandan PAC and its sister committee, the Committee on Commissions, Statutory Authorities and State Enterprises, have worked in close collaboration with Criminal Investigation Department police officers so that cases of financial wrongdoing that emerge from committee hearings lead directly to police investigations and many times to court cases.[16]

Table 1: The frequency that Commonwealth PACs achieve specific results

Results	Frequently achieved	Seldom achieved	Never achieved	Sample
Govt responds favourably to committee recommendations	69.4%	24.5%	6.1%	49
Govt implements committee recommendations	56.3%	37.5%	6.3%	48
Improvements in the integrity of govt information or databases	55.3%	34.0%	10.6%	47
Disciplinary action was taken against officials who contravene admin. guidelines	26.1%	34.8%	39.1%	46
Changes in legislation were adopted as a result of committee work	19.1%	63.8%	17.0%	47
Legal action was taken against officials who contravene laws	15.2%	41.3%	43.5%	46

Source: WBI Questionnaire on Scrutinising Public Expenditures in Commonwealth Parliaments.

15. G. C. Malhotra, 2000, 'Ensuring Executive Accountability: India's Public Accounts Committee', *The Parliamentarian*, April: 179–86.
16. World Bank Institute, 1999, *A Member's Handbook*. Report Based on a Parliamentary Workshop in Entebbe with the World Bank Institute and the Parliamentary Centre of Canada.

PAC Chairs were also asked what powers and practices they considered important in achieving results. When given a list of 37 potential success factors, most respondents considered most of the suggested factors to be 'very important'. However, when asked what the top three factors critical for success were, a consensus began to emerge, especially when Chairs were subsequently asked to identify important powers or practices that their committee did not have or follow but which would be useful to have. A selection of responses is summarised in Tables 2 and 3.

Table 2 shows that there was substantial agreement among respondents concerning the four powers – namely, the power to: (i) formulate recommendations and publish the conclusions; (ii) investigate all past and present expenses; (iii) choose topics without government interference; and (iv) compel witnesses to answer questions. An analysis of a larger sample of responses to the questionnaire than previously available suggests that a clear focus on financial accountability, rather than whether policies were good or bad, is not as important to PAC Chairs as previously thought – 54.9 percent thought it was very important in the latest analysis compared to 90.9 percent of the smaller sample used when preparing the 2005 PRWP. Nevertheless, for all five powers, more than 90 percent of Chairs rated them as 'very important' or 'somewhat important'.

The larger sample of responses suggests there is less agreement amongst PACs as to the importance for PACs of having the power to: (i) review the legislative auditor's budget; (ii) compel ministers to appear; and (iii) review proposed legislation or amendments to the Legislative Auditors Act. This differs from the analysis of the smaller sample used for the 2005 PRWP, which initially indicated that close to, or more than, 50 percent of PACs considered such that powers were 'very important'. However, it should be noted that the percentage of PAC Chairs who thought that these powers were not applicable to their circumstances was considerably higher than other powers, suggesting these are not powers universally enjoyed by PACs or powers actively sought by PACs.

Regarding composition of the committee, only two of the 37 potential success factors included in the questionnaire belong to this category. The first factor is the 'balanced representation of all major political parties in the commission', while the second factor is 'exclusion of government members from the commission'. There was again a high degree of consensus among respondents, with more than 80 percent reporting these factors as 'very important' and 75 percent believing that the exclusion of Members of Parliament with Cabinet posts was 'very important' or 'somewhat important'. Interestingly, 22.2 percent of the larger sample of respondents felt that the exclusion of government ministers from the PAC was 'not applicable', suggesting that the inclusion of ministers might not even be a possibility in a large proportion of the sample PACs, which indicates a potentially higher rate of ministerial exclusion than the statistics imply.

APPENDIX 3

Table 2: Importance of specific powers to Commonwealth PACs

Specific power	Very important	Somewhat important	Not important	Not applicable	Sample
Make recommendations and publish accounts	96.3%	3.7%	0.0%	0.0%	54
Investigate or review all past, current and committed expenditures of govt, organisations receiving funds from govt, and all state or Crown corporations	81.1%	9.4%	3.8%	5.7%	53
Choose subjects for examination without govt direction/advice	85.2%	14.8%	0.0%	0.0%	54
Clear focus on administration policy, and not on whether policies are good or bad	54.9%	39.2%	3.9%	2.0%	51
Compel witnesses to answer questions	83.3%	7.4%	3.7%	5.6%	54
Review the legislative auditor's budget	25.9%	18.5%	16.7%	38.9%	54
Compel ministers to appear before the committee	44.4%	11.1%	14.8%	29.6%	54
Review proposed legislation or amendments to the Legislative Auditors Act	33.3%	29.6%	9.3%	27.8%	54

Source: WBI Questionnaire on Scrutinising Public Expenditures in Commonwealth Parliaments.

Table 3: Importance of composition of the PAC to its success

Composition and membership	Very important	Somewhat important	Not important	Not applicable	Sample
Balanced representation of all major political parties on the PAC	81.5%	9.3%	1.9%	7.4%	54
Membership should exclude government ministers	68.5%	7.4%	1.9%	22.2%	54

Source: WBI Questionnaire on Scrutinising Public Expenditures in Commonwealth Parliaments.

With regard to committee practices and procedures, there was again a fairly strong consensus among respondents regarding success factors. As Table 4 indicates, these include the keeping of transcripts of meetings, adequate preparation before committee meetings, follow-up procedures on government action regarding committee recommendations and close working relations between committee members of different political parties. In essence, over 90 percent of respondents felt that these procedures and practices were either 'very important' or 'somewhat important' to the success of their PAC.

Table 4: Importance of practices and procedures to the success of Commonwealth PACs

Practices and procedures	Very important	Somewhat important	Not important	Not applicable	Sample
Transcripts kept of all hearings and meetings	85.2%	13.0%	1.9%	0.0%	54
Advance preparation of members before hearings	77.8%	18.5%	3.7%	0.0%	54
Effective follow-up procedures to determine if action has been taken to implement the committee's recommendations	68.5%	22.2%	7.4%	1.9%	54
Close working relationship between members from different political parties	74.1%	16.7%	5.6%	3.7%	54

Source: WBI Questionnaire on Scrutinising Public Expenditures in Commonwealth Parliaments.

3: SUCCESS FACTORS AND CONDITIONS FOR PACS

The top success factors and best practices, including some comments about why they are important and how they help achieve results for the PACs that suggested them are discussed below. This section also considers some reasons why these success factors might not be present, or why they do not work well in certain contexts. We have incorporated related success factors together, where appropriate.

3.1 Broad scope: the power to investigate or review all past, current and committed expenditures of government[17]

PACs enjoy a very broad mandate as they have the power to oversee all public expenditure, whether past, current or committed government expenditure. Such a broad mandate gives the PAC a vantage point with respect to a wide range of public services, and an entry point into the administration of many departments and agencies, even if other parliamentary committees are involved in their policy aspects. The wider the PAC's mandate, the greater the potential there is for the PAC to deter waste and wrongdoing and encourage better management of public resources.

Most PACs have this type of power; although some cannot examine committed expenditures, most can examine revenue administration. However, sometimes the full range of public functions is divided between the PAC and other financial oversight committees, such as a committee overseeing public enterprises or undertakings. Other possible limitations on the scope of PACs' mandates include restrictions on the ability of the PAC to investigate: (i) important institutions such as the central bank; (ii) important fields of public administration, like statutory expenditures, that are not voted on each year; or (iii) tax expenditures. In India, for example, the central government PAC is unable to probe into the workings of financial institutions or the central bank or the accounting policies and standards of government financial reporting, or the adequacy of existing auditing standards in the public sector.

Even with a broad mandate, there are situations that nullify or reduce the effectiveness of PACs. Some supporting factors and conditions which aid PACs to make the best use of a broad mandate are:

- having a specific permanent term of reference that permits the PAC to examine the public accounts and legislative auditor's report;
- legislative audit reports that detail the causes of problems, rather than just recounting the problems themselves;
- timely publication of the public accounts and legislative auditor's reports;
- co-operation of all committee members, especially those from the governing party – this ensures there is the political will in the PAC to both criticise the government's performance and to help it perform better;
- clear demarcation of responsibilities with other parliamentary committees;
- good support from the legislative auditor (but not too much dependence);
- effective planning and priority-setting process in the PAC; and
- adequate briefing, support and resources for identifying important issues.

17. Reasons given for selecting this success factor included: (i) 'Be perceived as the principal government watchdog'; (ii) 'To get details and the rationale behind government decisions'; (iii) 'Keeps a check on administration being slack, arbitrary'; (iv) 'Monitor fiscal discipline'; and (v) 'Effective check on finances'.

All these further conditions are important. For example, it is common, and important, to have a permanent term of reference to examine the public accounts and legislative audit reports. Through their examination of legislative audit reports, many PACs have the opportunity to examine broader questions relating to the economy, financial efficiency and effectiveness. Naturally, the ability to effectively examine these issues is dependent on the type of information provided by the legislative auditor and the attitude of the committee. Some committees are more comfortable dealing with instances of fraud, waste and abuse with brief audit notes about problems, rather than with broad value-for-money issues such as discussing systems weaknesses, policy specifications, legislative loopholes or cultural factors that caused the problems in the first place. As with all parliamentary committees, the preferences of the Committee Chair may be a contributing factor.

Another problem highlighted in the research was that sometimes the tabling of the accounts and audit reports are delayed, leaving the PAC to deal with old issues or without work until the documents are available; similarly, there are times when the heavy workload delays getting to the most current material. While some committees face a serious backlog of work, others have found ways to deal with this problem. Two responses provided by PAC Chairs to the survey questionnaire provide examples of different ways PACs are tackling the backlog of work.

Example 1:
'[In the past] the practice of the committee was to take [Comptroller and Auditor-General] CAG reports on a first-in first-out basis ... the reports of the CAG kept accumulating, resulting in a lackadaisical attitude on the part of government officials. Therefore, to improve the state of affairs ... the Committee now takes up recent reports, and accords paragraphs ... different priorities.'

Example 2:
'The Committee was able to finish a year's work in less than a year through regular meetings.'

Clearly, a move towards last in, first out (LIFO) may be a preferred option to the conventional first in, first out (FIFO) method of arranging deliberation of audit reports. Some terms of reference state or imply a detailed examination of the accounts, or a concentration on compliance rather than value for money.[18]

18. For example, Singapore and India, although in the case of India the PAC's mandate extends beyond compliance with rules and regulations to control over expenditure, its probity, wisdom and economy.

APPENDIX 3

Some committees interpret a permanent term of reference pertaining to the review of documents submitted to the committee as meaning they must systematically review all aspects of all reports, rather than selecting the most important ones. Others take the term of reference relating to the review of certain documents or reports as a limitation that they cannot examine anything else. However, most PACs set priorities and select important matters to examine within the scope of their mandate. Interestingly, sometimes PACS expand their purview to take a creative look at root problems, as was done in Case study 1.[19]

3.2 Free choice: the power to choose subjects for examination without government direction and advice[20]

The power to choose subjects for examination independent of government direction and advice provides the PAC with the freedom to focus on relevant and important matters. Having a broad scope mandate is of little use if the committee is unable to identify major issues or if the government directs the committee away from these. PAC Chairs reported that they are most effective if they can initiate inquiries on their own, as necessary, without having to wait for specific terms of reference from the government.[21] The elements of speed and even of surprise are often important here; if the committee can act quickly to select incisive issues, and if the choice and timing cannot be predicted by the government and the public service, the PAC's inquiries can have a deterrence effect.

Case study 1: United Kingdom

The United Kingdom PAC has ten government and six opposition members with an opposition member as Chair. It was established in 1861. It issues, on average, 10–20 reports a year based on the reports of the National Audit Office (NAO). The PAC sometimes looks beyond the audit reports to root causes of problems. For example, in 1994 it issued a groundbreaking report called 'the Proper Conduct of Public Business' that provided a broad checklist of improvements to help depart-

19. British Columbia (Canada) is another good example of a committee that works with their legislative auditor to identify important matters for follow-up.
20. Reasons given for selecting this success factor are: (i) 'Helped the ad-hoc committee work independently without government interference'; (ii) 'Issues rigorous reports and decides own agendas, inquiries'; (iii) 'Select matters of concern and hold government accountable'; (iv) 'Maintain independence'; (v) 'Undertake inquiries in areas of concern'; and (vi) 'Allow PAC to scrutinise all areas of government accountability'.
21. New South Wales (Australia) is an example where the PAC experienced more activity and enjoyed greater effectiveness once its mandate was changed to allow it initiate its own inquiries.

ments to avoid the failings in financial administration that had brought them before the auditors and the PAC in the past.

In 1999, the PAC asked the NAO to examine the Committee's impact. The NAO agreed, and provided a detailed, frank assessment for the committee's private information. The review identified and assessed three main aspects of the PAC's impact:

- the government's implementation of the Committee's recommendations;
- the views of senior public servants who were most often witnesses before the PAC and whose departments were the subject of its reports; and
- the quality of press coverage of PAC hearings and reports, as measured in various ways including coverage by leading journalists.

The assessment reviewed some known examples of PAC reports that had been implemented, including a recent follow-up report that convinced the government to abolish an agency.

This case illustrates a very close relationship between a PAC and a legislative auditor. Both have achieved useful results, some of which can be quantified. Although the review of the impact was not an independent study of the committee's effectiveness, it breaks new ground in the measurement of PAC performance.

Some committees focus primarily on specific audit notes or individual transactions uncovered by the legislative auditor. Relevant subjects for the PAC to focus on include looking beyond individual grants, contracts and other transactions to consider larger system weaknesses that make the individual problems inevitable. Committees should factor in the likelihood and practicality of the government taking corrective action on the subjects addressed. Consideration should also be given to whether the PAC is the most effective vehicle for dealing with an issue or whether other committees or institutions might be better placed to deal with the issue more effectively.

The selection of important and relevant issues by PACs depends on a number of supporting factors and conditions, some of which were identified and supported in the survey. Conditions conducive to PACs being able to select appropriate issues to focus on include:

- co-operation of all parties on the committee;
- clear focus on accountability, rather than on policy;
- effective research staff with knowledge of public administration and accountability;
- members with relevant experience;
- clear vision of improvements needed in public administration; and
- effective chairing.

If these conditions are missing; for example, if there is a highly partisan atmosphere, the committee's ability to choose subjects freely will be reduced.

With a government majority on most committees, some restrictions in the selection of issues to focus on are inevitable.

Having a clear focus on accountability is one way to instil a unity of purpose among different parties. Almost all PACs surveyed thought this was very important. For example, if all committee members can agree with the objective of holding the government accountable for spending, and for the stewardship of public assets, then the committee can focus on implementation of government programmes rather than policy matters, and focus on the accountability of civil servants for administrative and financial operations rather than on the political accountability of ministers. This will help at all stages of a committee's work – selecting issues, carrying out an inquiry and drafting a report. If all parties in the committee agree on a clear focus at the beginning of an inquiry, the Chair will have a much easier time keeping the committee on track towards a useful conclusion.

3.3 Effective analysis and reporting: the power to make recommendations and publish conclusions[22]

Virtually all committees value the power to make recommendations and report publicly. Most committees produce specific reports, with recommendations at the end of each inquiry, although not all inquiries can be brought to a successful conclusion in a single report. Some committees also produce an annual report and may request a debate in Parliament on specific matters. Some also require a response from the government within a set time.

In many jurisdictions, reports and recommendations follow closely those of the legislative auditor, and some depend on the auditor to follow up their recommendations.[23] Where both the PAC and the legislative auditor make recommendations, close collaboration and support of each other's work is essential. A division of labour that seems to be effective is when the legislative auditor reports on the status of government administration and performance of civil servants and the PAC adds a broader perspective of the political economy to this information by identifying the root causes and practical solutions.

The completion of a successful inquiry and report depends in turn on a number of conditions (some of which were identified in the survey as success factors):

22. Reasons given for selecting this success factor are: (i) 'Publish reports'; (ii) 'Seek government response'; (iii) 'Ensures implementation and review'; (iv) 'Allows committee to express itself'; (v) 'Forms basis for debate and follow-up'; and (vi) 'To ensure accountability to taxpayer'.
23. For example, in the United Kingdom, Canada, Ontario (Canada) and British Columbia (Canada).

- a focused inquiry with clear objectives (for example, in Australia the purpose of questioning witnesses in connection with a legislative audit report is not to analyse all the findings and recommendations in detail, but to seek action commitments that can be reported and then followed up);
- effective drafting procedures for reports;
- all-party agreement on the recommendations, to increase the likelihood of acceptance;
- good research and analysis support from staff; and
- effective follow-up procedures, to increase the likelihood of implementation.

One of these additional factors in particular received strong support from PAC Chairs – effective follow-up procedures. Follow-up is closely related to the power to make recommendations and publish conclusions because suggested improvements are of little use if they are not implemented. Surprisingly, two Chairs thought this was not important,[24] but most rated it 'very important' to encourage the government to act, and to track the committee's record and therefore effectiveness. The role PACs play in following up on their initial inquiries is highlighted in Case study 2.

Case study 2: Canada

The Committee on Public Accounts (PAC) of the Government of India is composed of 14 government and eight opposition members, with an opposition Chair. Committee members are elected from both Houses of Parliament. The PAC has been in existence since 1921 and is referred to as 'the eyes and ears of the legislature'. It generally produces more than ten reports a year, and works very closely with the Comptroller and Auditor-General, whose reports the PAC examines even before they are tabled in the House (although it cannot report on them until they are tabled). The PAC keeps track of recommendations implemented by the government – over 60 percent in the past 20 years, and more once the PAC follows up. An early example of an important accomplishment was the implementation of the PAC's 1947–48 recommendation to establish internal audit. Furthermore, on occasion the PAC has been known to initiate its own independent inquiries; for example, into tax evasion by a foreign bank.

The PAC usually examines a selection of the instances of unauthorised or extravagant expenditure and other cases which are raised in the auditors' reports. Sometimes these initial investigations uncover larger issues. One such instance was in 1993 and 1994, when a PAC report commented on the failure of India's Export Processing Zones to live up to expectations. The PAC was following up on previous recommendations aimed at helping these special zones meet their target of producing 8–10 percent of India's total national exports. In the 1980s, export zones had

24. South Australia (Australia) and Prince Edward Island (Canada).

contributed only 2–3 percent of total exports. The PAC was concerned to learn that for the period from 1991 to 1993 the rate of total exports from the Export Processing Zones was still in the 2–3 percent range. This was the case, despite the PAC issuing recommendations to improve the output of these special zones. In response to the PAC follow-up report, the government commissioned a special study to develop a strategy for attracting foreign capital and technology and improving export performance. The PAC may follow up again, although it has yet to do so. From past experience, the PAC claims that, on occasion, the announcement of its intention to hold further hearings has had a deterrent effect.

This case study illustrates an attempt by the PAC to deal with broader issues than what the PAC would normally deal with; namely, the fact that the results of an important government programme were not being monitored or reported adequately. The PAC has taken a high-level approach to the problem, focusing on the final result and leaving it to the government to decide on and monitor the means to improve export performance.

3.4 Solid technical support: from the legislative auditor and research staff

The diligence and skill of committee investigations depends on many factors such as bipartisan co-operation (see below), good chairmanship and the ability of individual members to probe reluctant witnesses. Underpinning the success of all of these factors is solid research support. Good advice and information is central to selecting important issues and pursuing them to a conclusion.

The legislative auditor is usually the chief support for the PAC – the 'friend, philosopher and guide', as one PAC Chair explained. In some cases, the legislative auditor sits with the committee,[25] provides staff directly to the PAC or performs work otherwise done by PAC staff. The PACs in our survey had an average of fewer than two professional staff assigned full time, but the range was wide, falling between 0 and 22 permanent staff. These numbers could include professional staff providing procedural advice and report-drafting skills. The responses to the questionnaire or interviews did not highlight any cases where research had been contracted out; however, this probably happens. Surprisingly, two of the survey respondents thought that relations with the legislative auditor was not important, while three thought the use of outside expertise and research support was not important. Most others gave these factors a high rating, though.

A PAC needs research skills and resource to obtain and analyse information and testimony, especially when the committee decides to tackle difficult issues.

25. For example, in India and Ontario (Canada) the legislative auditor is allowed to ask questions of witnesses.

In some countries outside the Commonwealth, a more adversarial relationship exists, with witnesses being examined by the legislative auditor, who acts as a 'court of accounts', or by members of the PAC with legal help and more judicial powers. In most Commonwealth PACs, though, 'fair play and decorum' usually prevails. This can be contrasted with some other PACs, such as the US congressional committees, which witness life-and-death partisan battles. The need for legal training and help in cross-examining witnesses seems to be less important in Commonwealth countries, although there are examples where it has been important, such as in Case study 3.

Some factors or conditions that help create solid research support for committees include:

- excellent communication skills, especially the legislative auditor who has to translate financial and technical material into lay terms for the PAC;
- adequate resources for expert staff and advisers, independent expert witnesses, and perhaps for travel and public hearings;
- a level of trust between staff, experts and committee members, in particular the assurance that staff are non-partisan; and
- a good relationship between researchers and the public service and/or strong access to information laws and regulations.

Perhaps surprisingly, lack of resources was not mentioned too often as a problem – the survey results are not conclusive on this point.[26] The survey did not provide sufficient information on the value added by outside expertise or how often independent witnesses testify, although the findings are clear that all committees value/need strong research support.

Case study 3: Canada

Earlier this decade, the federal PAC in Canada had nine government and eight opposition members with an opposition Chair. It produced 10–20 reports a year based mainly on the reports of the Auditor-General of Canada. The PAC also conducted inquiries on its own, such as investigating international financial reporting standards for the public sector, and internal audit and evaluation. The government pays close attention to PAC recommendations and has already implemented those made a few years ago as a result of another independent inquiry supporting more frequent reporting by the Auditor-General.

26. It is logical to assume that resources were the key variable here, but the questionnaire responses did not highlight any correlation between the number of committee professional staff and the results committees reported achieving. The United Kingdom, one of the most effective committees, has only one professional staff member. The questionnaire did not collect any information on how many staff or other resources legislative auditors provide to PACs, though.

An excellent example of the work of the Canadian PAC is the inquiry into the activities of Atomic Energy of Canada Limited (AECL); although it is now somewhat dated, it is nevertheless an informative example. This case concerns an independent PAC investigation about 25 years ago, beginning with a short reference in the Auditor-General's report to unsubstantiated payments made by AECL, a Crown corporation. The PAC conducted a detailed inquiry into more than C$20 million that AECL had paid to agents abroad in hopes of selling nuclear reactors it manufactured. The PAC concluded that AECL followed totally unacceptable business practices and reported that they suspected some of the payments were used for illegal or corrupt purposes. The PAC went far beyond the audit report, wrote many letters, called many witnesses, including the retired company President, held 17 hearings over the course of a year, and wrote a far-reaching report that recommended major changes in the accountability regime for Crown corporations that were subsequently implemented. During the course of the inquiry, all committee members actively cross-examined hostile witnesses. The media gave the inquiry front-page attention and were able to uncover further evidence the PAC could not have obtained on its own.

This case illustrates a number of features of an effective PAC; namely, the ability to select important issues, a focused inquiry that was tenaciously pursued, and a big-picture report with recommendations that were implemented.

3.5 Bipartisan climate

Strong disagreements between and/or within political parties can be very damaging to the PAC. Parliaments are, by definition, arenas for the clash of ideas, and it is not surprising that differences of principle and even partisan issues in the legislature can carry over into the PAC. Sometimes the partisan differences reach a point where the government is unwilling to accept any criticism or to act on valid complaints, and the opposition, for its part, overplays minor misdemeanours.

Some of the survey respondents alluded to partisan problems. Having a balanced representation among parties within the committee most Chairs thought was 'very important' and five respondents identified it among their top three success factors. Developing a close working relationship among members from different political parties also applies. Most Chairs thought this very important, although none identified it among their top three. Another factor contributing to a bipartisan climate is having a clear focus on implementation of policy, and not on whether policies are good or bad.[27]

27. In one response to the questionnaire a PAC Chair expressed the view that there is a need for flexibility when dealing with important matters of public concern regardless of the demarcation between policy and implementation. This view is based on the notion that policy is effective only to the extent that it can be implemented.

Is a close balance of party representatives on the committee important, rather than a large government majority? There are examples of effective PACs with large government majorities, but this undoubtedly places more pressure on the need for skilled and experienced opposition representation and chairmanship. This would be more difficult in Parliaments with only a few opposition members as the opposition would have a difficult time serving on the PAC as well as other parliamentary oversight committees.

The survey suggested that the United Kingdom and Australia have been quite successful in defusing partisan disagreements. There are checks and balances built into these models – opposition Chair but government majority; focus on administration but not policy; focus on public servants and not ministers (in United Kingdom only) – that help to work around partisan problems and make it adaptable to varied situations. In addition there are special factors in the United Kingdom Parliament that support committee work as a career path, including the longer tenure of Members of Parliament on the committee and the large number of Parliamentarians who cannot hope to become government ministers. The United Kingdom PAC also declines to mediate between the legislative auditor and the government in disputes about the facts of a case, thus eliminating one cause of partisan friction in the committee and avoids time-consuming discussions about *whether* something happened, rather concentrating on *why* it happened and *what has been done* to prevent it happening again.

In Australia (federal and state Parliaments), the Committee Chairs – most of whom are government members – place great emphasis on operating in a non-partisan manner and on reaching unanimous agreement about agendas and reports. But unlike in the United Kingdom, the federal PAC in Australia also deals with disputed issues between the executive branch and the legislative auditor. This PAC is able to select a wide range of issues of public accountability on a non-partisan basis regardless of whether the issue is raised in the Auditor-General's report.

Interviews provided some further suggestions for diffusing partisan disagreements. The suggestions included:

- reducing ministerial involvement both as members and as witnesses (but having *former* ministers may provide valuable experience);
- sometimes a minority government or close balance of parties in the legislature heightens partisan tensions in the PAC, while at other times it creates the need for co-operation. One would expect a minority government to tolerate or compromise on administrative issues that don't threaten to become election rallying points;

APPENDIX 3

- sometimes an experienced and skilled chair can develop strategies to avoid or minimise partisan deadlock. In-camera meetings to set agendas and review or draft reports help;[28] and
- sometimes election by the legislature of the Committee Chair, provision of a special salary and/or other perquisites can increase the prestige of the position and make it attractive to politicians who might otherwise seek more partisan rewards.

In short, while there is no panacea for tempering the partisan climate, it can sometimes be reduced by the changes discussed above and by other means, such as clearly focusing on accountability for implementing approved policy objectives without questioning the objectives themselves.

3.6 Public involvement and media coverage

There are regional differences in the extent of public involvement in the PAC and parliamentary affairs generally and opinion is divided on whether the media should have access to PAC meetings. However, there are examples where the media has provided valuable information for a PAC inquiry (see Case study 3) and there is anecdotal evidence to suggest that the presence of the media may also keep public servants and auditors on their toes and help precipitate realistic government commitments in response to PAC investigations.

Case study 4: New South Wales (Australia)

The PAC of New South Wales, Australia, has three government and three opposition members, with the Chair from the governing party. It was established in 1902, but its powers were significantly increased in the early 1980s, with bipartisan support. At

28. The recent European Union study of Supreme Audit Institutions (SAI) and Parliamentary Committees (PC) identified six factors that help prevent politicisation of audit-related meetings: (i) the organisation of the parliamentary committee's work according to the Parliament's Standing Orders; (ii) the participation in PC meetings of officers responsible for the matters being discussed, and other experts; (iii) the participation in PCs of members from all political parties and the right of all members to be heard; (iv) the oath each Member of Parliament takes which provides for adherence and respect for the Constitution and other legislation; (v) in some of the countries the Members of Parliament endeavour to avoid politicising PC sittings when the SAI-related matters are discussed; and (vi) in case of committees that are, exclusively or mainly, in charge of state audit-related issues, the position of a chairman is sometimes held by a representative of an opposition party (the Czech Republic, Malta, Poland) or a representative of an opposition party holds the position of a vice-chairman.

that time it began to initiate its own inquiries and hold public hearings, supported by its own secretariat and working closely with the Auditor-General.

This case study focuses on several PAC inquiries into the justice system. Increasing caseloads and litigation have burdened many of the agencies that participate in the justice system in New South Wales, including the police and court system. The end result, for the public, was a feeling of powerlessness and concern about the quality of justice and about serious delays in the courts. In 1995, the Auditor-General conducted a preliminary audit of the performance of the court system. The PAC decided to focus on one aspect of the subject on which Parliamentarians had a special vantage point – the impact of the system on the public. It invited briefs from interested parties, held public hearings and generally sought to engage the public in its deliberations. The PAC published a bipartisan report with many recommendations to improve the court experience for the public.

Since then, many changes, several government inquiries and a follow-up audit have taken place. There have been big improvements in waiting times for criminal cases in the Supreme and District Courts, and case management procedures and time standards have been introduced. However, the rapid growth in civil cases has continued to cause problems. As such, in 2001, the PAC began another public inquiry. By focusing this time on the results achieved by the courts in the context of the justice system as a whole, they attempted to ensure that bottlenecks are removed, not just moved. Their report was published and it recommended broad changes, including greater use of alternative dispute resolution, compulsory mediation, and penalisation of legal practitioners who unnecessarily delay civil cases.

This case takes a system-wide look at a problem from the public's perspective. In doing so it illustrates a useful and inexpensive way to involve the public directly in a PAC inquiry that builds on the work of the legislative auditor but does not rehash it. It also illustrates a tenacious follow-up programme that builds credibility for the PAC's future work.

Committees in the 'developed Commonwealth' (Australia, Britain, Canada and New Zealand) tend to meet in public, while elsewhere the practice is mixed. Committees in South Asia generally do not meet in public, but the committees in Jamaica, Singapore and South Africa do, as did the ad hoc committees in Pakistan between 1999 and 2002. The argument that is made in South Asia is that secrecy facilitates frank exchanges with witnesses. However, the PACs in these countries are no more successful than in other jurisdictions, undermining this claim.

In Rajasthan, India, great strides have been made in opening up the budget process to public input. However, there does not appear to be any corresponding move to open up PAC meetings to public. The same situation occurs in Orissa and Karnataka in India. The United Kingdom PAC is also somewhat reticent to open its proceedings to the public; until 1977, the PAC met in camera and still does not hear outside witnesses. Nevertheless, there are some reforms designed to encourage public involvement in the budgeting process in the United Kingdom. Furthermore, there are alternate avenues through which the public can provide direct feedback on government services, specifically through the Citizen's Charter. In fact, the emphasis on published performance measures in Australia, Canada and the United Kingdom involves the public directly by seeking their assistance in assessing the quality of service delivery. Closer direct contact between the executive and the public is not inconsistent with public involvement in the PAC, and can provide new and relevant information to help the PAC hold the government to account.

Certain powers can be useful when seeking to draw upon the public's knowledge and experience when performing the PAC's functions, notably the power to subpoena witnesses and to hold witnesses in contempt of Parliament if they fail to answer questions. Where such power is lacking, the glare of publicity can compensate for the lack of specific power. However, as outlined in Case study 5, in circumstances where PACs or the Auditor-General lack the authority or power to undertake their inquiries effectively, Parliament can extend the remit of these institutions through passage of additional legislation.

Case study 5: Ireland

The PAC has operated since the foundation of the State in 1922 and both it and the Office of Comptroller and Auditor-General (CAG) are modelled on their United Kingdom equivalents.

In early 1998 media reports suggested there might be significant evasion of Deposit Interest Retention Tax through the use of bogus non-resident bank accounts. The total amount of money held in non-resident bank accounts was in the billions of pounds, much of it legitimate. The PAC sought to investigate the matter but concluded it had insufficient powers to do so. This led to the enactment of the Comptroller and Auditor-General and Committees of the Houses of the Oireachtas (Special Provisions) Act 1998, which granted extensive quasi-judicial powers to the CAG and allowed him to investigate the operation of the tax by the revenue authorities and the financial institutions and to report his findings to Parliament. This investigation broke new ground and the CAG's report formed the basis for a subsequent public inquiry by a sub-committee of the PAC into the whole affair, which generated enormous public interest. It led ultimately to the payment of significant sums by the financial institutions and others to the revenue authorities. The affair significantly raised public awareness of the PAC and the Office of the CAG.

Some committees, for example in Australia, Ireland[29] and Canada, tend to accept testimony from outside experts as well as the general public, rather than relying totally on the legislative auditor and public servants. The PAC in New South Wales, Australia, is a particularly good example of this trend because it considers public education as one of its primary responsibilities, and often picks subjects for examination that benefit from direct public input, such as the level of service that the government provides. In general, PACs that do not meet in public, or accept input from the general public or particular interest groups, are missing a key source of information that likely hinders their effectiveness.

3.7 Summary

The factors or conditions PAC Chairs consider are most important for the conduct of a successful committee include:

- having a broad scope or mandate;
- possessing the power to select issues without government direction;
- power to report conclusions, suggest improvements and having the resources and ability to monitor and follow up on their recommendations;
- strong support from the legislative auditor, PAC members and research staff, which creates a unity of purpose around the PAC's work;
- developing a professional bipartisan relationship among PAC members; and
- involving the public and encouraging media coverage.

It should be noted, however, that the possession of these powers or the presence of these factors does not guarantee success, nor does their absence necessarily hinder PAC effectiveness. The responses to the questionnaire highlighted a number of common problems which inhibit the success of PACs. These include the failure of some PACs to hold regular meetings or to write reports, the failure to keep up to date with the reports of the legislative auditor, or the propensity of some PACs to focus too much attention on superficial issues. When considering the constraints on the operation of particular PACs it is pertinent to ask why certain powers have not been granted, or, if granted, are not used by some PACs. By looking at the broader environment in which legislative oversight takes place, it is possible to learn more about why some PACs work better than others.

One determining factor when it comes to understanding the success of certain PACs is the willingness of government to allow Parliament in general, and the PAC in particular, sufficient political space to carry out their constitu-

29. Ireland is not a Commonwealth country, but has a Westminster parliamentary system.

tional mandates. There are several interrelated problems, which play into the hands of a government that wishes to curtail the effectiveness of the PAC. First, there are the inherent weaknesses of parliamentary committees and of Parliamentarians, and the lack of commitment on the part of some governments in correcting these weaknesses. Secondly, there is the perception that given the history of an adversarial relationship between the auditor and those who are being audited, the 'findings' of the legislative auditor are too negative and not always sufficiently balanced, therefore should not be given a specific forum in Parliament where they can be championed. Furthermore, the information deficit that usually exists between the members of the PAC and the government-backed public officials whom they are seeking to hold accountable can intimidate members of the PAC. The lack of information, depth of knowledge or diligence amongst Members of Parliament may create a self-fulfilling prophecy, whereby Parliamentarians fail to use the PAC to engage the government effectively and the government loses respect for the role of legislative oversight.[30]

Despite these obstacles, there is a growing realisation that an effective PAC is central to open, accountable and responsive governance. As such, there is a growing trend amongst Commonwealth countries[31] to strengthen the role of Parliamentarians and parliamentary committees, including PACs.

4: BENCHMARKS FOR MEASURING PAC PERFORMANCE

At present there is no international standard setting process for legislative functions such as oversight and control of the public purse. It is not surprising that public sector accounting and auditing is perceived to have fallen behind the total quality management exhibited in the private sector, despite advances in the quality of public auditing. The gap between the public and private sector financial accountability standards and practices is likely to grow given there is no existing impetus to address this critical issue. However, there are some encouraging signs. For example, international auditing associations have set some international audit standards and Auditors-General have already made considerable progress in improving and standardising quality public auditing services.[32] Unfortunately, the same cannot be said for PACs, where the development of standards has been uneven and slow.

30. In Australia, the PAC did not meet for almost 20 years from 1932–51 because the government decided it was unnecessary.
31. Namely the United Kingdom, Canada and Australia and, more recently, in countries such as Ghana, Kenya, Sri Lanka and Uganda.
32. International Organisation of Supreme Audit Institutions (INTOSAI), Strategic Plan 2005–2010.

4.1 Measurement framework for PACs

This appendix seeks to add to the debate about the content of benchmarks that could be used to measure the overall performance of PACs. Below is a broad preliminary framework, encompassing three benchmarks, which could be used as a starting point for a fuller debate on the best way to measure the effectiveness of PACs around the globe.

(i) *Benchmarks for determining the level of* **activity**
This indicator seeks to measure events and the extent of resources used in the operation of PACs, such as:

- the extent to which a PAC keeps up to date with legislative auditor's reports; and
- the cost (monetary/time) of delivering outputs, such as operating budget, time of staff, members, witnesses, and so on.

(ii) *Benchmarks for determining the level of* **output**
This indicator seeks to measure the immediate visible results of the work of the committee, such as:

- the frequency with which the PAC issues reports;
- recommendations made by the PAC;
- what the PAC does to follow up and monitor the implementation of the recommendations it makes; and
- the extent to which the PAC's recommendations have been implemented.

(iii) *Benchmarks for determining the extent of* **outcomes**
This indicator seeks to measure the durable improvements in public administration that can be attributed to its output, such as:

- increased efficiency or effectiveness of government programmes;
- better compliance by public officials with laws or regulations;
- improvements in financial and control structures, such as prosecution of wrongdoers and stronger powers for the legislative auditor;
- more accurate and timely flow of government information to the PAC and into the public domain;
- enhanced public awareness of government programmes; and
- enhanced legislative knowledge about the quality of public management of programmes and resources.

All three dimensions of performance are important. In addition to these three broad preliminary indicators, the issue of whether a specific

PAC is actually dealing with important issues such as the root causes of systemic problems, rather than the symptoms (like corruption) needs to be contemplated. In addition, it would be beneficial to consider the deterrent effect the PAC has on the behaviour of public servants. This dimension of performance has been coined 'relevance'[33] and could constitute an additional indicator of success. There is a growing interest amongst PACs in measuring their effectiveness and performance. The Quebec Committee on Public Administration is an example of a relatively new PAC that is seeking to evaluate its effectiveness (see Case study 6).

Case study 6: Quebec (Canada)

The Committee on Public Administration (CPA) in Quebec has six government and four opposition members, with an opposition Chair. The CPA took over from the former PAC in 1997 with new responsibilities that stressed administrative, non-partisan action as well as a review of the Auditor-General's reports. The CPA reports twice a year.

In 2002, the Chair of the Committee started an informal review of the first five years of the committee's work by asking six key questions:

- Could the CPA make the distinction between political and administrative aspects in the management of departments and agencies?
- Could senior public servants testify without getting their political masters into hot water?
- Could a bipartisan approach work in the CPA given the highly partisan nature of the legislature?
- Does the legislature permit the CAP to hold timely public accountability sessions with departments?
- Will the CPA be able to review the many new performance reports that departments are required to produce each year?
- Has the CPA ensured that its recommendations and the government's action plans to deal with their recommendations are followed up effectively?

The Chair of the CPA presented this framework for a PAC scorecard at the 2002 meeting of all Canadian public accounts committees. Initially, he made his own preliminary personal assessment of the CPA's score for each question/criterion, with the intent of involving the full CPA in a more formal assessment with the results tabled in Parliament.

This case identifies most of the key problems that PACs face in achieving effective results. Moreover, it illustrates a courageous attempt by a PAC to assess its own effectiveness.

33. Our thanks to Bob Miller, Executive Director of the Parliamentary Centre, for pointing us in the direction of an IDRC publication on *Organizational Assessment, a Framework for Improving Performance* that suggests relevance as an indicator.

The research conducted for this appendix uncovered very few published reports by a PAC that deals with its own performance. This is somewhat surprising considering performance reporting is an important feature of effective parliamentary oversight and some PACs already review and critique departmental performance reports or performance reports prepared by Auditor-General. Despite the lack of published reports on the performance of PACs, there are some examples of best practice that could be emulated around the world. The Victorian Public Accounts and Estimates Committee is such an example (see Case study 7).

Case study 7: Victoria (Australia)

The Australian state of Victoria has had a Public Accounts and Estimates Committee (PAEC) since 1895. Its members are senior, high-profile Parliamentarians; five of whom are from the government side (including the Chair) and five are opposition members. It has three main objectives: to encourage economic, efficient and effective utilisation of public resources; to enhance accountability to Parliament and the public; and to enhance the presentation and disclosure of information to Parliament and the public. In part, because of its estimates responsibilities, the PAEC is more active than most PACs, averaging over 50 meetings a year.

The PAEC has very wide responsibilities, which include initiating and carrying out its own inquiries. To help it with its broad mandate the PAEC has a panel of specialist advisers that deal with complex and technical issues. In addition, the PAEC works closely with the Office of the Auditor-General. They frequently suggest changes to the terms of reference for performance audits and selectively follow up on unresolved issues in its reports. The PAEC also recommends the appointment of the Auditor-General, and commissions a performance audit of the legislative audit office every three years. An interesting and possibly unique activity is the programme of seminars that the committee holds for Members of Parliament on financial and accountability subjects.

The PAEC has carefully thought through what it would like to achieve and how to achieve the objectives the committee set for itself. Its annual report contains a chart depicting what the PAEC does and the impact of its work. This performance and results framework starts with the inputs – the knowledge and skills of members and the information received from stakeholders about the operations of government – and the outputs, which are advice and recommendations. It then moves into a detailed analysis of the intermediate outcomes– such as better performance of government – and finally outcomes such as improved public confidence and better parliamentary control. In the same report, the PAEC publishes performance targets and plans for the year, as well as statistics on past performance. Thus, for example, the PAEC sets a target for the government's acceptance of its recommendations, and it keeps count and publishes the results. It also keeps track of the timeliness of its review and coverage of the Auditor-General's reports, and is not afraid to report slippage if they do not finalise all the work they expected to do. The PAEC is a leader in performance reporting for PACs.

In part, the reluctance of PACs to assess their performance is a result of the difficulty in quantifying the information needed to respond to, even the most obvious, benchmarks. Also, it should be noted that focusing on measuring the successes of PACs could have perverse effects, such as possibly encouraging a PAC to select easily resolvable issues or make soft recommendations. There is a danger that a PAC might shy away from difficult but valuable work with long-term impact if that impact cannot be measured in the short term or at all. PACs should be diligent in ensuring they do not undermine their impact for the sake of meeting performance benchmarks. Despite these concerns, performance reporting ultimately provides an opportunity for PACs to gain an insight into how they are operating and whether they are generating the outcomes and impact they desire.

5: CONCLUSION

In his study of Public Accounts Committees and Auditors General, McGee (2002) identifies three main priorities for action. First, the institutional capacity of Parliaments, PACs and of Auditors-General needs to be enhanced so that they are able to fulfil their oversight functions. According to McGee, building the capacity of these institutions can be achieved by increasing staffing and resources, training and access to information. Secondly, McGee emphasises that a key determinant for the success of Auditors-General is their independence from partisan and political influence. Auditors-General need to have the freedom to carry out their duties independently and impartially. Finally, McGee stresses that in order to be effective PACs need to operate in an environment where there is a free flow of information. Specifically, PACs need to exchange information and ideas in order to stay up to date with developments, changing standards and best practices as they emerge.

The evidence presented in this appendix is, to a large extent, consistent with the conclusions formulated by McGee. The PACs Chairs surveyed in the study conducted by the WBI reported that information availability and bipartisanship/non-partisanship are critical conditions for the success of the PACs. However, the analysis contained in this appendix outlines more fully how the capacity of PACs can be improved so that they can better undertake their financial accountability function. Two sets of factors seem of great importance in this regard. One concerns the institutional design of the PAC, while the other concerns its behaviour and functioning.

The success of the PACs depends to a large extent on how they are modelled or institutionalised; more specifically, the powers PACs are imbued with and their mandate. First, this appendix suggests that PACs should focus on governments' financial activity and accountability rather than evaluating or assessing the content of the governments' policies. Secondly, this appendix argues that PACs should have the power to investigate all past and present government expenses regardless of when they were made. Thirdly, PACs should be given the power to check whether the government actually undertakes some steps to implement the recommendations made by the PAC. Finally, PACs must have a close working relationship with the Auditors-General.

The success of the PACs does not depend exclusively on their institutional design; the behaviour of its members and the functioning of the PAC are equally as important. Drawing upon the responses to the questionnaire, this appendix has been able to identify some obvious best practices. First, the PACs' members must seek to act in a non-partisan manner and should try to develop a good working relationship with other committee members, in spite of possible partisan differences. As an extension of this, the PAC should always strive for consensus when making decisions and issuing recommendations. Secondly, the effectiveness of the PAC improves whenever its members study the documentation provided by the Auditor-General and public officials and generally prepare themselves for PAC meetings. Finally, PACs should maintain a transcript and record of their meetings, publish their conclusions and recommendations, and encourage the public and the media to participate in its deliberations. Public opinion can, in fact, provide a strong incentive for governments to improve their financial accountability and avoid possible allegations of ineffective management.

Based on the feedback received from over 50 PACs in Asia, Australasia, Canada and the United Kingdom, this appendix argues that there are certain features that can potentially improve the performance of PACs. Accordingly, an ideal PAC would have the following components:

- the PAC should be small: committees seem to work well with five to eleven members, none of whom should be government ministers;
- senior opposition figures should be associated with the PAC's work, and probably chair the PAC;
- the Chair is a senior Parliamentarian, fair minded and respected by Parliament;
- members of the PAC should be appointed for the full term of the Parliament;
- the PAC should be adequately resourced, with an experienced clerk and a competent researcher(s);
- the PAC's role and responsibilities are clear and well-understood;
- the PAC meets frequently and regularly;

APPENDIX 3

- hearings are open to the public, and a full verbatim transcript and summary minutes are quickly available for public distribution;
- a steering committee plans the PAC's work in advance and prepares an agenda for each meeting, which is distributed to all members of the PAC;
- the typical witness who attends before a PAC should be a senior public servant (the 'accounting officer') accompanied by the officials that have a detailed understanding of the issues under examination;
- the Auditor's report is automatically referred to the PAC and the Auditor meets with the members of the PAC to go over the highlights of the report;
- the PAC occasionally decides to investigate matters, independent of the issues raised by the Auditor-General;
- the PAC strives for some consensus in its reports;
- the PAC issues formal substantive reports to Parliament at least annually;
- the PAC has established procedures with government for monitoring the implementation of its recommendations and is informed about what, if any, action has been taken;
- in all its deliberations, the PAC uses the Auditor as an expert adviser; and
- Parliaments hold an annual debate on the work of the PAC.

Index

Audit 94–99
Auditor-General 62, 69, 95–99, 105, 110–114, 127

Budget
 amendment 49, 67–68, 77–82, 128–130
 approval 35–36, 45–51
 forecasts 15–16, 28
 meaning 1–5
 preparation 7–10, 16–23
 presentation 36–39
 secrecy 31–34
 strategy 26–30, 40
 timing 37–38, 50–51

Committees 68–77, 103–112
Congressional Budget Office (USA) 7, 63, 80, 111
Confidence, votes of 46–49

Election reporting 89
Estimates 41–43, 45, 49, 57–59, 71–77

Federal systems 117–121
Fiscal responsibility 10–12

Gender budgeting 12–15, 40–41
Government Accounting Office (USA) 111

Impoundment 84
Interim expenditure authority 55–57, 59–60

Loans 52–53

Millennium Development Goals 26–27

Outputs and outcomes 43–44, 127

Parliamentary Budget Office (Uganda) 20–21, 30, 64, 73, 80
Participatory budgeting 23–26
Public Accounts Committee 62, 65–66, 69, 72, 98, 103–106, 109–114, 125
Public–private partnerships 53–55, 97, 106–107

Reporting 87–89, 99–104, 120
Reversionary budgets 59–60

Supplementary budgets 57–59
Scrutiny unit (UK) 65
Second chambers 50, 117, 121–124

Unappropriated expenditure 113–115

Virement 57, 89–91